KATE ANDERSEN

WELFARE THAT WORKS FOR WOMEN?

Mothers' Experiences of the Conditionality within Universal Credit

POLICY PRESS SHORTS RESEARCH

First published in Great Britain in 2023 by

Policy Press, an imprint of
Bristol University Press
University of Bristol
1–9 Old Park Hill
Bristol
BS2 8BB
UK
t: +44 (0)117 374 6645
e: bup-info@bristol.ac.uk

Details of international sales and distribution partners are available at
policy.bristoluniversitypress.co.uk

British Library Cataloguing in Publication Data
A catalogue record for this book is available from the British Library

ISBN 978-1-4473-6638-6 hardcover
ISBN 978-1-4473-6639-3 ePub
ISBN 978-1-4473-6640-9 ePdf

Cover design: Liam Roberts Design
Front cover image: PantherMedia/agsandrew
Bristol University Press and Policy Press use environmentally responsible print partners.
Printed and bound in Great Britain by CPI Group (UK) Ltd, Croydon, CR0 4YY

FSC
www.fsc.org
MIX
Paper | Supporting responsible forestry
FSC® C013604

In loving memory of my mum, Jan Denison (1956–2021)

Contents

List of tables and figure

Tables

Figure

List of abbreviations

AET	Administrative Earnings Threshold
CET	Conditionality Earnings Threshold
CSJ	Centre for Social Justice
DWP	Department for Work and Pensions
JCP	Jobcentre Plus
JSA	Jobseeker's Allowance
MIF	minimum income floor
QLR	qualitative longitudinal research

About the author

Kate Andersen is Research Associate at the University of York. Her research explores the intended and unintended consequences of new social security policies. Kate is especially interested in investigating how government justifications for social security reforms compare with the everyday lives of people in receipt of social security benefits. Her research particularly focuses on how social security reforms impact women. She has published an article titled 'Universal Credit, gender and unpaid childcare: mothers' accounts of the new welfare conditionality regime' in *Critical Social Policy* (2020).

Acknowledgements

First and foremost, very many thanks to the mothers who took part in this study. This research would not have been possible without their willingness to share their experiences and views with me. I really appreciate their time and their open and thoughtful answers to my questions. Many thanks also to the numerous individuals and organisations who helped with recruiting participants to the study.

The research reported in the book greatly benefited from input from my two PhD supervisors, Peter Dwyer and Aniela Wenham. They provided an ideal and invaluable combination of challenge and encouragement and gave generously of their time, knowledge and support throughout the research. Likewise, many thanks go to my PhD examiners, Jane Millar and Nick Ellison, for their helpful comments and questions on my work. Thanks also for warmth and support in various forms to other members of the Department of Social Policy and Social Work and the Resource Centre for Social Sciences at the University of York, particularly Roy Sainsbury, Ruth Patrick, Christine Skinner, Caz Snell, Charlie Lloyd, Sharon Grace, Debbie Haverstock and Denise Munday.

It would have been difficult to complete the research without the childcare my parents provided, but more than that I am so grateful for their constant love and support. Lastly, to my children, Mae and James – I could not be more thankful for you.

ONE

Introduction

> Our antiquated welfare system has become a complicated and inflexible mess. It has been unable to respond to our evolving job market and the changing nature of our workforce.
>
> Society has changed but the benefits system has failed to change with it.
>
> So it is time to bring welfare into the 21st Century. We want a system which isn't seen as a doorway to hopelessness and despair but instead as a doorway to real aspiration and achievement. (Duncan Smith, 2010)

> Support is seeping away as Universal Credit is rolled out to more people. The way that Universal Credit has been designed and implemented appears to be based around an idealised claimant and it has features that are harming many, particularly the most vulnerable. Universal Credit can disadvantage women, disabled people and BAME people. (Economic Affairs Committee, 2020, p 3)

When Iain Duncan Smith, the then Secretary of State for Work and Pensions, gave his introductory speech on Universal Credit, he claimed that the UK social security system was deeply flawed and that Universal Credit was a 'fundamental welfare reform' that would reduce poverty (Duncan Smith, 2010). Given long-standing issues with the legacy benefits system, the ideas behind Universal Credit, and specifically the aims to simplify the benefits system and make work pay, initially received widespread support (for example, Sainsbury, 2010; Citizens Advice, 2011; Work and Pensions Committee, 2012). However, as the phased roll-out of Universal Credit has gathered pace, it has come under increasing criticism (for example, National Audit Office, 2018; Alston, 2019). As an Economic Affairs Committee report published in 2020 notes, the design and delivery of Universal Credit give rise to harm. There is mounting evidence that attests to the multiple ways in which Universal Credit can cause significant hardship to those claiming it (Wright et al, 2018; Cheetham et al, 2019; Patrick and Simpson, 2020; Robertson et al, 2020; Wickham et al, 2020). This is particularly problematic given that Universal Credit is a far-reaching new social security benefit: in 2018 it was estimated that when fully implemented, Universal Credit will affect just under seven million households (Kennedy and Keen, 2018).

One aspect of Universal Credit policy which has attracted criticism is the new conditionality regime for main carers of children (termed 'lead carers' in the government literature). As Dwyer explains, conditionality within the social security system 'links eligibility to continued receipt of work related benefits to claimants' mandatory engagement with work-focused interviews, … training and support schemes and/or job search requirements' (2018b, p 142). Conditionality is enforced by benefit sanctions (the reduction or complete withdrawal of benefit payment for perceived noncompliance with work-related requirements). Under the conditionality regime within Universal Credit for lead carers, the parent with the primary responsibility for the care of dependent children is subject to different levels of work-related requirements (depending on the age of the youngest child). While subjecting single parents to conditionality is a continuation of previous policy, Universal Credit policy considerably intensifies and expands the previous conditionality regime and also removes many exemptions single parents previously had the right to. The changes brought about by Universal Credit are particularly significant for coupled main carers of children: the implementation of Universal Credit extends work preparation and job search requirements to these claimants for the first time. Although Universal Credit policy is purportedly 'gender neutral' and men and women are treated the same under Universal Credit (DWP, 2012c, p 23), according to government impact assessments, the changes to conditionality for single parents and the main carer in couples are expected to predominantly affect women (DWP, 2011a, 2012c, 2015c).

This book focuses on the impacts of this new conditionality regime on women's everyday lives as well as the wider implications for the UK social security system and women's position in the dominant citizenship framework. Prior to the research presented in this book, gender concerns had been raised that this regime devalues unpaid care,[1] weakens women's position in the paid labour market and limits their agency regarding engagement in unpaid care and paid work (for example, MacLeavy, 2011; Cain, 2016; Millar, 2019). However, there was a lack of research investigating whether and how the concerns were experienced and viewed by mothers subject to the new conditionality regime. The research presented in this book was born out of my concern for what this policy might mean for mothers, particularly given the pre-existing devaluation of women's unpaid caring roles,

1 The term 'unpaid care', rather than 'unpaid care work', has been used throughout this book. While unpaid care entails work, it is distinctly different from work as it also has a relational and affective orientation. Additionally, defining unpaid care as work essentially entails using a masculine concept to describe an activity primarily carried out by women and, therefore, risks imposing on women a male individualist concept of work that may contradict their own understanding of their activities, relationships and identities (Ribbens McCarthy and Edwards, 2002).

women's disadvantaged position in the paid labour market and the historical ways in which women have been denied agency. I considered these issues particularly important as they all relate to women's routinely precarious citizenship status (see Chapter Two). I was also motivated by the desire to explore not only whether the gender concerns were realised in the lives of women subject to this policy but also the ways in which Universal Credit policy brought about any gendered impacts. Therefore, I conducted research which aimed to explore over time how the new conditionality regime affects mothers' caring roles and responsibilities, their employment trajectories and their agency concerning engagement in paid work and unpaid care. To meet these aims, I carried out a qualitative longitudinal study in 2018–19 which investigated the views and experiences of mothers subject to the conditionality regime for lead carers of children within Universal Credit. Through analysis of the empirical evidence generated in the fieldwork, this book demonstrates the considerable gendered impacts of the conditionality within Universal Credit. More broadly, it shows that the conditionality constitutes a significant shift in the UK's social security system that exacerbates women's marginalised position in the dominant gendered citizenship framework. Ultimately, this book calls for social security benefits to be designed and delivered in ways that enhance, rather than undermine, women's citizenship status and practice.

Austerity context

Universal Credit has been introduced in the context of a programme of austerity implemented by the Conservative–Liberal Democrat Coalition government (2010–15) and the subsequent Conservative governments (2015, 2017 and 2019). While this programme of austerity nominally ended in 2018 and there was a dramatic increase in government spending due to the COVID-19 pandemic, many of the social security measures introduced during the period of austerity remain.

The austerity programme involved making cuts to working-age public social expenditure ostensibly to reduce the public sector deficit but also to alter the role and size of the welfare state (Taylor-Gooby, 2012; Edmiston, 2018). Therefore, alongside the introduction of Universal Credit, there have been several other key changes to the social security system which have increasingly affected Universal Credit claimants (Economic Affairs Committee, 2020). Key social security reforms have included introducing a benefit cap, a two-child limit and a benefits freeze (Kennedy et al, 2017). The benefit cap was introduced in 2013 and reduced in 2016. It limits the total amount of benefits a household can receive. The two-child limit was introduced in 2017. Under this policy, families no longer receive child elements in tax credits and Universal Credit for third or subsequent children born on or after 6 April 2017. From 2016 to 2020 there was a freeze on the value of most working-age benefits, including Universal Credit. Over the past decade there have also been some increases in the generosity of the social security, wage and tax systems, such as the increase in personal tax allowance, the introduction of the National Living Wage and the increase in help towards formal childcare costs. However, those who benefit the most from the introduction of the National Living Wage and the increased personal tax allowances are not necessarily the same individuals who experience reductions in income due to cuts to Universal Credit and tax credits (De Henau, 2018).

There are gendered impacts of austerity policies (MacLeavy, 2011; Rubery and Rafferty, 2014; Durbin et al, 2017). Women have been disproportionately affected by public spending cuts in social security benefits, including Universal Credit, as they are more likely to be in receipt of such benefits (Rubery and Rafferty, 2014; Richards-Gray, 2020). A key reason for women's reliance on social security benefits is their disproportionate responsibility for unpaid care (Richards-Gray, 2020). For example, the majority of single parents are female, and single parenthood particularly gives rise to receipt of social security benefits (Conaghan, 2009; Reis, 2018). Analysis by the Women's Budget Group found that by 2021/22, employed single mothers in receipt of Universal Credit will lose on average £4,933 per year if changes to the tax, wage and social security systems are assessed together, and unemployed single mothers will lose £7,000 per year (De Henau, 2018, p 4). Therefore, the introduction of the new conditionality regime within Universal Credit has taken place in the context of gendered social security reforms which have weakened women's social protection.

Motivation for the book

The main motivation for writing this book is to present empirical research which shows how mothers' lives are impacted by the new conditionality within Universal Credit, from their perspective. This is particularly important given that mothers' voices have historically been seldom heard and that qualitative research investigating claimants' experiences and views was sidelined during the policy formation of Universal Credit (Bennett and Sung, 2014). Based on the experiences and views of mothers subject to the conditionality within Universal Credit, this book aims to provide recommendations for Universal Credit policy and practice. However, there is also a wider aim of contributing to the ongoing discussion about gender, the social security system and women's citizenship. As highlighted in this book, there has been a shift in social security policy wherein women are increasingly expected to undertake paid work. This has devalued women's unpaid care work and has not been accompanied by a recognition of the women's disadvantaged position in the paid labour market. Therefore, this book seeks to illustrate the problems with this shift and to further thinking on how the social security system can recognise and value women's unpaid work and improve their position in the paid labour market, in part by enlarging women's agency concerning their engagement in paid work and unpaid care.

Researching mothers' experiences

To investigate how the conditionality within Universal Credit affects the valuing of unpaid care, women's employment trajectories and women's agency, I carried out a qualitative longitudinal study. I conducted two rounds of semi-structured interviews with a group of mothers subject to the conditionality within Universal Credit. This explored over time their experiences of and views on this new conditionality regime. Qualitative longitudinal research (QLR) entails qualitative enquiry conducted over time (Neale, 2012) and typically involves making repeat and comparative observations of participants' actions and views (Saldaña, 2003; Smith, 2003). QLR is primarily concerned with analysing change (Corden and Millar, 2007; Neale, 2015) and consequently is particularly useful for discerning how people experience, manage and respond to change, and how change impacts people's lives (Neale and Flowerdew, 2003; Neale, 2015). Given that the implementation of conditionality for lead carers within Universal Credit represents a significant policy change and the empirical research was concerned with investigating the impacts of this policy, QLR was an appropriate research design to employ. In addition to giving insight into what change occurs and why, QLR is helpful for uncovering the absence of change, which may be significant (Saldaña, 2003; Lewis, 2007). Consequently, QLR was helpful in exploring instances in which participants did not experience change as a result of the implementation of conditionality for lead carers (see, for example, Chapter Five). This research strategy was also appropriate given the aim within Universal Credit to change claimants' behaviours and attitudes towards paid work. Corden and Millar explain, 'This focus on change [within QLR], both on how people change and on how people respond to change, is very relevant in the current policy context in which individual behaviour change is seen as key to achieving desired policy goals' (2007, p 529). Therefore, QLR was useful for observing the salience of the theory of change within Universal Credit (see Chapter Three) and specifically whether the conditionality for lead carers changed attitudes and behaviours towards paid work, and, ultimately, employment trajectories (see Chapters Five and Six).

A further purpose of QLR is to obtain more detailed insight into participants' experiences (Saldaña, 2003). Through repeat waves of qualitative data collection, a richer and more nuanced understanding of participants' accounts can be obtained (Thomson, 2007; Miller, 2015; Neale, 2015). This is particularly pertinent in the study of social security services, as people's experiences of and responses to such services develop over time as people have multiple interactions with services and experience the consequences of earlier interactions (Lewis, 2007). The two waves of interviews conducted for this study generated data that provided a fuller account of the ways in which the conditionality within Universal Credit impacted on the mothers' caring responsibilities, employment trajectories and agency.

The location of the study was Yorkshire, England, and the majority of the participants were recruited from the city of York. Universal Credit was fully rolled out in York in July 2017, and therefore the city had a sufficient number of claimants to recruit from when the fieldwork started in September 2018. Locating the study in this city provided a contrast with other studies investigating similar themes (for example, Graham and McQuaid, 2014; Patrick, 2017) as the city has a lower unemployment rate than the national average. From April 2018 to March 2019 – when the first wave of interviews took place – the unemployment rate in York was 3 per cent, whereas the national average was 4.1 per cent (ONS, 2019c). Therefore, this study provides insight into how conditionality affects mothers in an area where there are ostensibly greater job opportunities. However, while York has a low unemployment rate, it also has significant inequalities. For example, while it has a number of high-value sectors such as bioscience and financial services, which pay high wages, it also has a skew towards sectors such as tourism, retail and care, which pay low wages and offer limited opportunities for progression (City of York Council, 2016). There are also big differences in child poverty rates and life expectancy between the city's wards (York Human Rights, 2018). In addition, it is regarded as an unaffordable place to live due to the high housing costs (Walker, 2018). Consequently, the economic context of York is more complex than may initially appear.

To select participants with experiences of and views on the conditionality for lead carers within Universal Credit, the following primary sampling criteria was used: participants had to be mothers (single or in a couple) in receipt of Universal Credit who were subject to either work preparation or job search requirements. While only three of the mothers had a joint claim for Universal Credit at the first wave of interviews, a further three had previous experiences of a joint claim and one had experience of a joint claim between the two waves of interviews. Therefore seven accounts of the joint claim were obtained. The participants were recruited through a variety of means and an information leaflet was used to aid the process. Strategies included recruiting participants through gatekeepers (for example, at housing associations, a homeless hostel and organisations that help get people into paid work), placing an advert on a local website for mums, visiting community centres and using a Facebook account that was set up specifically for the purpose of the study. The resultant sample comprised 24 mothers.

To obtain the mothers' accounts of the conditionality within Universal Credit, I carried out semi-structured interviews. The first wave of interviews took place between September 2018 and March 2019, and the second wave took place between June 2019 and November 2019. Several strategies were adopted to maintain the sample over time, including sending Christmas cards, notecards and a summary of the findings from the first wave of interviews. On recontacting the participants, I was able to get in touch with all but one. I contacted this participant's link person, who told me the mother had suddenly moved from the study location and had cut off contact with everyone from it. The other 23 participants agreed to be interviewed again. However, three participants asked to rearrange the planned interviews and did not respond to subsequent phone calls and texts. Therefore, 20 participants were interviewed a second time. I used thematic analysis to analyse the data and the analysis was conducted both cross-sectionally after each interview and longitudinally once both waves of interviews were complete. All of the data was analysed, regardless of whether the participants took part in a second interview (Corden and Nice, 2007).

Throughout the research, careful attention was given to conducting the study in an ethical manner, and the potential impact of the research on the participants was particularly considered (Elliott, 2005). The research adhered to the British Sociological Association's (2002) ethical guidelines. Key ethical issues prioritised included informed consent, confidentiality and anonymity, prevention of harm and reciprocity. At the end of the study, to provide an accessible output for the participants and the stakeholders they wanted to influence, I worked with a graphic designer to develop a leaflet outlining the main research findings and policy recommendations. This was sent to policy makers, politicians, charities and other stakeholders who had expressed an interest in the findings during the research.

Structure of the book

This book provides the background to the research, reports on the findings and discusses the policy recommendations and wider implications for women's citizenship arising from the study. Chapter Two discusses gender and the social security system, and explains the dominant gendered concept of citizenship. It then presents a more gender-inclusive citizenship framework and explains how valuing unpaid care, promoting paid work and affording women agency is crucial to creating this more inclusive framework. Chapter Three turns to the policy context of the study. It starts by exploring the history of Universal Credit, the contested aims and assumptions underpinning it, and its design and delivery. The chapter then gives a brief history of conditionality in the UK before detailing the Universal Credit conditionality regime for lead carers. It ends by presenting the gender concerns that have been raised regarding this new conditionality regime.

Chapters Four, Five and Six present analysis of the original data generated in the qualitative longitudinal fieldwork. Chapter Four details the implications of the conditionality within Universal Credit for the valuing of unpaid care. It explores the extent to which caring responsibilities were taken into account during the participants' Universal Credit claims, the effects of the conditionality within Universal Credit on the mothers' caring responsibilities and their views on whether unpaid care is valued within the Universal Credit system. Chapter Five explores the implications of the conditionality within Universal Credit for women's position in the paid labour market. It discusses the participants' paid work aspirations and barriers to paid work, the formal childcare provision within Universal Credit, the support participants received in obtaining paid work, and the participants' experiences of trying to meet paid work requirements. It then investigates the effects of the conditionality within Universal Credit on the participants' employment and earnings over time. Chapter Six focuses on the effects of the conditionality within Universal Credit on mothers' agency. It investigates the extent to which the participants' work-related requirements were negotiated, their experiences of the compulsion within Universal Credit over time and their views on the compulsion. The chapter then explores the participants' responses to the compulsion within Universal Credit and the overall impacts of the compulsion on their agency regarding engagement in unpaid care and paid work.

Chapter Seven concludes the book. After summarising the overall research findings, it discusses the implications of the conditionality within Universal Credit for women's citizenship and the social security system. It then outlines the arising policy recommendations for the Universal Credit conditionality regime, which are aimed at promoting a more gender-inclusive citizenship framework. This chapter concludes by articulating how the conditionality within Universal Credit exacerbates women's disadvantaged citizenship status, and highlighting the importance of seeking and incorporating the views of claimants when devising social security reform.

TWO

The social security system and gender: unpaid care, paid work and agency

Introduction

Women routinely hold a disadvantaged position in the UK social security system. This position is related to the dominant gendered concept of citizenship in the UK. The gendered citizenship framework in the UK marginalises and excludes women, and attempts to create a concept of citizenship that is more inclusive of women have encountered difficulty. This chapter details gendered aspects of the 1940s welfare reforms, shows how demographics have changed considerably since these reforms were introduced and explains that there has also been a shift in the UK social security system's treatment of women, with women increasingly expected to undertake paid work. It then shows that a key dilemma facing feminists seeking to create a more gender-inclusive citizenship framework is whether to position women as 'workers' or 'carers', and discusses the difficulties with the social policies that arise from these two different routes to citizenship. The chapter ends by describing a more gender-inclusive citizenship framework and explaining how policies can be implemented that help develop this framework, with a specific focus on the importance of promoting women's agency.

Gender social security and changing demographics

Historically, and currently, women have held an inferior position in the UK social security system (Lister, 2003; Pascall, 2012). The Beveridge reforms of the 1940s have particularly attracted criticism for the gendered assumptions underpinning them (Sainsbury, 1996; Pascall, 1997, 2012; Lister, 2000b). These criticisms show a lack of recognition of the ways in which the post-World War Two welfare state was beneficial to women (Blackburn, 1995); nevertheless, the welfare reforms established a social security system that was based on masculine interactions with the paid labour market (Lister, 2001), which resulted in inferior social security rights for women. For example, there was an assumption that men would undertake paid work and women would be responsible for unpaid care and domestic labour (Sainsbury, 1996; Pascall, 1997). While Beveridge described women's unpaid care as 'vital work' (1942, p 53), under the welfare reforms and most notably the National Insurance Act 1946, men made contributions through paid employment, and when husbands were unemployed, benefits were paid to them on behalf of their wives (Pascall, 1997). Single parents were provided for under the National Assistance Act 1948; however, these social security payments were considerably lower than the contributions-based payments of the National Insurance Act. Additionally, while women did receive Family Allowance (a flat-rate payment funded from taxation for the second and subsequent children), this was not enough to provide economic independence for mothers and children (Pascall, 1997). Therefore, while historically there has been some recognition of mothers' caring roles in the form of unconditional social assistance granted on the basis of their caring responsibilities (Daly, 2011; Davies, 2015), this has been at an inferior level (Orloff, 1993; Lister, 2003). In the UK social security system, wage earners have been privileged over unpaid carers, resulting in second-class social rights for many women (Lister, 2003).

Due to significant changes in family demographics and women's increased participation in the paid labour market, the contemporary societal context is very different to that of the 1940s when the post-World War Two social security system was established. Over the past 30 years, there has been an increasing diversity of family forms, including blended families (Falkingham et al, 2014). Since the 1950s, there has been a decrease in marriage rates, with couples increasingly opting to cohabit (ONS, 2020). There has also been an increase in the divorce rate, particularly since the 1970s, following on from changes in divorce law (Rafferty, 2014). The increase in divorce rates along with the increase in births to women who have never married have led to increases in single-parent families (Falkingham et al, 2014). The birth rate in England and Wales has fluctuated over the past 70 years, and after a peak in 2012, the birth rate for 2018 was the lowest ever recorded (ONS, 2019a). Changes in fertility rates by age group indicate that women are progressively delaying childrearing to older ages (ONS, 2019a).

The demographic changes since the 1940s have been accompanied by changes in women's participation in the paid labour market. Since the 1970s, women have increasingly entered paid employment (Roantree and Vira, 2018). There was a particular rise in the women's employment rate in the 1980s, and it has risen almost continuously since then (Roantree and Vira, 2018). However, despite women's increasing participation in the paid labour market, considerable gender inequalities are prevalent (Nightingale, 2020). Persistent gender inequality in the labour market is evidenced by the gender pay gap and the disproportionate representation of women in precarious jobs, which do not confer social security rights (Grant, 2009; Bowlby et al, 2010; Jensen and Møberg, 2017). Women are more likely to be in occupations that are associated with low pay, such as caring, cleaning and catering (Reis, 2018). Some feminists have argued that such work is poorly remunerated and undervalued because it is viewed as 'feminine' and therefore presumed to be inferior (see, for example, Fraser, 1998; Lynch and Lyons, 2009). Within occupations, women are also underrepresented in higher-level positions that pay more (Reis, 2018) and are less likely to progress to higher-paying work (D'Arcy and Finch, 2017). Additionally, women are increasingly undertaking self-employed work, which is often accompanied by low pay, limited options for training and a lack of social protection (De Henau et al, 2018). Mothers are particularly susceptible to a disadvantaged labour market position: while women earn about 10 per cent less than men before they have children, the gender pay gap increases rapidly for many women after they have children (Costa Dias et al, 2018). Despite demographic and labour market changes, and some slight shifts in men's engagement in unpaid care, women remain disproportionately responsible for unpaid care (Boyer et al, 2017; Jupp et al, 2019; Neitzert, 2020). Consequently, mothers are more likely than fathers to fit their working hours around caring responsibilities (Orloff, 2009; Bennett and Daly, 2014) and have a greater propensity to be economically inactive or to engage in part-time work (Bennett and Daly, 2014; Reis, 2018). Part-time work in the UK tends to be low paid, low status, insecure and segregated into gendered occupations, and results in inadequate pensions and limits career development (Williams, 2001; Lister, 2003; Rafferty and Wiggan, 2017).

Apart from motherhood, other demographic characteristics (such as class, ethnicity and disability) intersect with gendered inequalities to produce different experiences among women. Whereas middle-class women have tended to move into reasonably well-paid occupations and professions, working-class women have entered less well-paid, more precarious jobs (McDowell and Dyson, 2011). Racial discrimination and bias also compound gender inequalities: women from Black and

1759–97), whereby there are two seemingly incompatible routes for obtaining full citizenship status. The first route entails demanding full and equal access to the paid labour market so that women can obtain citizenship status on the same terms as men, through paid employment. The second route entails seeking citizenship status based on women's unique responsibilities, and demands that unpaid care is valued as highly as paid work. Differing emphases have been placed on the two routes.

The dominant feminist approach to improving women's citizenship status is to work within the existing framework and, therefore, to encourage women's participation in the paid labour market (Jensen and Møberg, 2017). Arguments in favour of this approach centre on the importance of paid work to women's economic security and independence. This is clearly important to single mothers who may not have access to a male wage, and it is also important to coupled mothers. Economic dependence on men can result in power imbalances in couple relationships (Orloff, 1993; Lister, 2000a). This can lead to a sense of deference and obligation and a lack of bargaining power in family decisions (Hobson, 1990; Lister, 2000a). This power imbalance may also affect the amount of control women have over the household resources and render them more vulnerable to poverty, which may remain invisible due to the measurement of poverty at the household level (Lister, 2003). Economic dependence on men can also reduce women's ability to exit unsatisfactory and abusive relationships, because such a move may result in poverty (Hobson, 1990). Engaging in paid work is also important for securing economic independence in later years given the decreasing levels of state-provided pensions and the increasing necessity of accruing an occupational pension.

While the social security system can and does provide a measure of economic independence to women, and particularly single parents, through the provision of child-related social security benefits, these have generally been at low levels, only enabling women and their children to exist in relatively deprived conditions (Orloff, 1993; Walby, 1994). In addition, Walby (1994) argues that the development of social rights through the welfare state represents a shift from a private to a public patriarchy. As a result, some women have exchanged dependence on men for dependence on the state. While this has been important for changing gender relations between men and women, it still renders women subject to control. Of particular relevance to the increasing implementation of conditionality in the UK (see Chapter Three), the advantages of economic independence obtained through social security provision depend in part on the way in which the state exercises power over those in receipt of benefits. Young explains, 'People who depend on public subsidy or private charity to meet some or all of their needs must often submit to other people's judgments about their lives and actions – where they will live, how they will live, how they will spend money, what they will do with their time' (1995, p 549). Thus, some see participation in the paid labour market as a preferable route in women's pursuit of economic independence (Orloff, 1993).

In contrast to the dominant feminist approach, in seeking to create a more inclusive and comprehensive citizenship framework, other feminists, such as Knijn and Kremer (1997), Sevenhuijsen (2000), Tronto (2001) and Pateman (2005), argue that citizenship needs to be redefined to recognise the importance of care so that engaging in unpaid care confers citizenship status. This argument is primarily made on the grounds that every citizen both gives and receives care at some point in their lives. All humans need care when they are young, and many will need it during old age and when seriously ill (Knijn and Kremer, 1997; Pateman, 2005). Care is not only universal and necessary but also highly valuable. For example, good care enables humans to flourish (Sevenhuijsen, 2000; Lewis and Giullari, 2005). It can affect people's ability to contribute in various spheres of life and relate to others (Lynch and Walsh, 2009). As Williams notes,

'In providing and receiving care and support in conditions of mutual respect we learn and enact the practical ethics of being attentive to others: responsibility, trust, being adaptable and accommodating to others' differences, toleration for our own and others' frailty, and how to sustain and repair relationships' (2004, p 76). In addition to this social contribution, provision of unpaid care also makes an economic contribution to society, both directly through saved government childcare costs and indirectly through the reproduction of the future labour force (Innes and Scott, 2003; Conaghan, 2009). Figures from the Office for National Statistics (2018) show that unpaid childcare in the UK was worth £352 billion in 2016.

A recognition of interdependency is crucial to establishing the value of care (Lynch and Lyons, 2009). Some feminists have been highly critical of the view that independence, conceptualised in terms of economic self-sufficiency, is a prerequisite for citizenship, and of the labelling of men as 'independent' due to their participation in the paid labour market and women as 'dependent' on account of their financial dependence on men (Pateman, 1989; Fraser and Gordon, 1994; Young, 1995; Knijn and Kremer, 1997). Within citizenship frameworks, there has been a lack of attention to the ways in which men and the state are dependent on women. Historically, men have relied, and continue to rely, on women's unpaid domestic and caring activities in order to undertake paid work (Pearce, 1990; Tronto, 2001; Pateman, 2005). Thus those engaging in the paid labour market only gain 'independence' due to their dependence on those who carry out unpaid care (Pearce, 1990). Likewise, the welfare state has relied on women for providing care for young, elderly and disabled people, and ensuring the continual reproduction of the labour force (Pateman, 1989; Holloway and Pimlott-Wilson, 2016). This has resulted in a paradox wherein women with caring responsibilities have been marginalised in citizenship frameworks for failing to contribute through paid work when, in fact, their nonparticipation in the paid labour market has been on account of the unpaid welfare work they undertake (Pateman, 1989; Cass, 1994). As a result, there are demands for dismantling the dichotomy between men's 'independence' and women's 'dependence' and for recognition of interdependency so that the contributions women make are valued and their citizenship status is elevated (Pateman, 1989; Young, 1995).

Potential policies for creating a more gender-inclusive citizenship framework

The dilemma regarding the two routes for pursuing women's citizenship remains problematic. As Lister explains, 'a tension exists between the value I want to place on unpaid care work as an expression of citizenship responsibility and the emphasis I give to the importance of women's labour market participation to their citizenship' (2003, p 177). Different policies arise from the two options. Improving women's position in the paid labour market involves closing the gender pay gap, addressing gendered horizontal and vertical occupational segregation and promoting women's access to quality paid employment alongside state provision of quality childcare (Orloff, 1993; Cass, 1994; Lister, 2003; Annesley et al, 2010). On the other hand, recognising and valuing unpaid care requires the provision of caregiver allowances (Pateman, 2005; Gillies, 2007; Lynch and Walsh, 2009). The different routes for pursuing women's citizenship and their accompanying policies have limitations.

While improving women's access and position in the paid labour market may reduce female poverty and increase women's economic independence and power, this approach also has deficiencies. Promoting women's participation in the paid labour market as a central route for women to obtain citizenship status requires women to conform to a citizenship framework which is based on men's attributes, abilities and interactions with the paid labour market (Pateman, 1989; Fraser, 1998; Lister, 2003). This approach therefore has the potential to devalue care

(Fraser, 1998), and it may not be possible for women to obtain full citizenship status: if they pursue this route, women may only obtain citizenship status as 'lesser men' (Pateman, 1989, p 197). This is in large part due to women's disproportionate responsibility for unpaid care and the impossibility of fully commodifying care. For historical and biological reasons, women are likely to continue to undertake more unpaid care than men (Fraser, 1994). Therefore, women will always be disadvantaged in the paid labour market, as all of women's responsibility for unpaid care cannot be transferred to formal childcare provision. For example, parental responsibilities such as attending to family emergencies, including child injury and illness, cannot be catered for by formal childcare provision (Fraser, 1998). The affective dimension of care also puts limits on the extent to which it can be commodified. Care is not merely a task: it also entails relationships, morals and emotions. Many mothers define 'being there' as an integral part of care (Ribbens McCarthy and Edwards, 2002), indicating that care is also about emotional and practical availability. Thus, while formal care plays an important role in supplementing unpaid care, it can never fully substitute for it (Lewis and Giullari, 2005; Lynch and Walsh, 2009).

Policies seeking to elevate the value of care, if implemented independently of measures to improve labour market equality and redistribute care, may also be problematic. For example, while caregiver allowances can elevate the intrinsic value of care and accommodate women's activities into citizenship frameworks rather than insist women conform to men's interactions with the paid labour market, they also have the potential to disadvantage women. A first concern is that providing caregiver allowances entrenches women in traditional gender roles, thereby reinforcing women's role as unpaid carers and men's role as earners in the paid labour market (Cass, 1994; Williams, 2004). This could impede a more even distribution of caring responsibilities and reduce women's capacity for agency regarding engagement in paid employment and unpaid care.

Low-income mothers in precarious jobs, in light of the nature of their paid employment, may particularly become entrenched in traditional gender roles due to the attractiveness of caregiver allowances (Bergman et al, 2012). The provision of caregiver allowances may also have negative implications for women's long-term economic position (Lister, 2003; Williams, 2004). Withdrawal from the paid labour market to look after children can result in decreased earnings over the life course (Orloff, 1993) and low pensions in retirement (MacLeavy, 2011). Time away from the labour market can also make re-entering paid work at a later stage difficult because of loss of knowledge of the contemporary labour market and loss of human capital and confidence (Grant, 2009). Therefore, pursuing citizenship status solely through policies such as caregiver allowances that aim to elevate unpaid care may further embed both women's disproportionate responsibility for care and their weaker labour market position.

Other means of creating a more gender-inclusive citizenship framework have been proposed, but these also have both advantages and disadvantages. For example, in order to both recognise the importance of care to citizenship status and promote women's labour market position, authors such as Orloff (1993), Cass (1994), Fraser (1994), Lister (2003) and Williams (2012) argue for the redistribution of care from women to men, thereby addressing the gendered division of labour. This is very advantageous in that it would free women to participate on a more equal basis with men in the paid labour market while also ensuring that caring responsibilities are attended to. However, such a position continues the devaluation of care by implying that women must participate in the paid labour market in order to achieve citizenship status and that men's engagement in unpaid care is necessary for it to be valued and recognised. Also, as Lister (2000a) and Orloff (2009) acknowledge, there may be practical limitations with this approach. Male participation in unpaid care may not be appropriate or possible – for example, in the case of abusive relationships. Consequently, while this solution may be beneficial for many mothers, other mothers may not see any improvement in their citizenship status as it would leave them dependent on men engaging more fully in unpaid care, which may be neither possible nor desirable. The next section discusses a more comprehensive means of creating a more gender-inclusive citizenship framework.

A potential way forward: valuing unpaid care, promoting paid work and enlarging agency

The varying approaches discussed for advancing women's citizenship status all contain both advantages and limitations. While the tensions in creating a more gender-inclusive citizenship framework render a solution that is free from disadvantages unobtainable, a promising way forward is to support both women's participation in the paid labour market and their roles as unpaid carers (Cass, 1994; Lister, 2003). The choice between promoting women's participation in the paid labour market and valuing their unpaid care needs to be dismantled as it represents an unhelpful dichotomy: both are valid expressions of citizenship (Lister, 2003). By improving women's position in the paid labour market and legitimising women's unpaid care, women's citizenship status can be promoted rather than hindered (Lister, 2003), particularly as this approach does not position women as solely 'workers' or 'carers' and, therefore, accommodates both the life course and women in their diversity. The policy ramifications of this approach would involve designing and implementing a wide range of measures aimed at supporting unpaid caring roles through the provision of time and financial resources, combating gendered inequalities in the paid labour market and redistributing unpaid care to men and the state where possible (Cass, 1994; Lister, 2003; Pascall, 2012).

Enlarging women's agency is key to creating a more gender-inclusive concept of citizenship. Agency refers to the ability to determine one's own daily life (Annesley, 2007) and relates to the capacity for free choice (Gould, 1983; Lister, 2003; Wright, 2012; McNay, 2016). However, agency is exercised within a social context and is influenced by social norms, interpersonal relationships, environments and relations of power (Wright, 2012; McNay, 2016). Therefore, while agency has the potential to promote freedom of choice, the ability to exercise choice is always constrained to some extent (Lister, 2004). Agency is key to citizenship and is particularly important to women's citizenship (Lister, 2003). It is crucial for empowering women and for ensuring women are not assumed to be passive dependents who fulfil ascribed social roles (Nussbaum, 2003; McNay, 2016). However, historically women have been denied agency, and it has been assumed that they are incapable of acting autonomously (McNay, 2016). Regarding unpaid care, while women have been assumed to be natural carers and ascribed the duty of care, Marshall's influential concept of citizenship did not include the right to give and receive unpaid care (Knijn and Kremer, 1997). This has the potential to limit women's options for carrying out care. As Knijn and Kremer explain, 'Only when both the right to give and the right to receive care are assured can citizens (caregivers as well as care receivers) have a real choice about how they want to integrate care in their lives' (1997, p 333). In addition, due to women's disproportionate responsibility for unpaid care, women are more limited than men in their ability to make unconstrained choices in regards to participation in the paid labour market (Lewis and Giullari, 2005). Thus, women are restricted by differing factors in their agency regarding engagement in unpaid care and paid work.

These constraints have the potential to devalue unpaid care (through failing to legitimise it and support it by not guaranteeing the right to care) and to limit women's participation in the paid labour market, and are incompatible with a citizenship framework that considers both paid work and unpaid care as valid citizenship contributions. Therefore, these constraints need to be addressed and women's agency needs to be enlarged, in part by implementing policies that help provide the material and social conditions that enable women to enact agency (Gould, 1983). Additionally, policy needs to be supportive rather than prescriptive, which is particularly important given the diversity of families (Duncan and Smith, 2002). Therefore, policies are required that not only promote the valuing of unpaid care and women's position in the paid labour market but also enable women (and men) to make genuine choices regarding engagement in unpaid care and paid work (Lewis and Giullari, 2005).

Conclusion

Women have a marginalised position in the UK social security system, and this is related to the dominant gendered concept of citizenship (based around masculine activities, attributes and interactions with the paid labour market). However, devising and implementing policies that help create a more gender-inclusive citizenship framework has encountered difficulty. The two main routes to pursuing women's citizenship status contain both significant advantages and disadvantages for women. These tensions are not easily overcome, but a promising way forward is to implement a wide range of policies designed to promote the value of unpaid care and women's equitable participation in paid work, and enable women to exercise agency regarding their engagement in unpaid care and paid work. This approach does not negate all of the tensions involved in women's citizenship dilemmas, and there is a much broader context in which gendered cultures and practices and other structural intersecting inequalities need to be addressed. However, this approach would give women different options for pursuing citizenship status (through paid work, unpaid care or a combination of the two) and therefore accommodate both the life course and the diversity of women. It would also rebalance the social security system so that it gives considerably more recognition to the unpaid caring activities disproportionately carried out by women. Additionally, through addressing gender inequalities in the paid labour market and providing adequate financial provision for those who engage in unpaid care, this approach would help ensure women's economic independence from men. However, the gender concerns raised in relation to the conditionality within Universal Credit (for example, MacLeavy, 2011; Whitworth and Griggs, 2013; Cain, 2016) suggest that this policy may further the dominant gendered citizenship framework. The next chapter discusses Universal Credit and presents the concerns raised about the new conditionality regime regarding women's roles as unpaid carers, their position in the paid labour market and their agency.

THREE

Universal Credit and the new conditionality regime for mothers

Introduction

Universal Credit was introduced to reorient the social security system around paid work. It aims to increase entry and progression in paid work, in part through intensifying and expanding conditionality. One means of increasing conditionality was to introduce a new conditionality regime for lead carers of dependent children. Numerically, women are disproportionately affected by this new regime. This chapter outlines the history, aims, design and delivery of Universal Credit. It then gives a brief history of conditionality in the UK before detailing the Universal Credit conditionality regime for lead carers. The chapter ends by presenting gender concerns that have been raised in relation to this new conditionality regime.

History of Universal Credit

Universal Credit has its origins in the Centre for Social Justice (CSJ), a think tank founded by Iain Duncan Smith in 2004, aimed at addressing the root causes of poverty (Haddon, 2012; Duncan Smith, 2017). Following an investigation into five perceived causes of poverty (family breakdown, educational failure, worklessness and economic dependence, addictions, and indebtedness), the CSJ started looking at options for simplifying the benefits system (Haddon, 2012). The CSJ then undertook detailed modelling of a single benefits system and, in further work with David Freud, devised Universal Credit. The opportunity to implement Universal Credit arose when Duncan Smith was appointed Secretary of State for Work and Pensions following the 2010 election. In 2010, the Department for Work and Pensions (DWP) published a Green Paper entitled '21st century welfare' (DWP, 2010a), which outlined five options for simplifying the benefits system; however, it was clear that Duncan Smith and the DWP favoured Universal Credit (Sainsbury, 2010; Timmins, 2016). Universal Credit was then incorporated into the October 2010 Spending Review. In November of the same year, the DWP published 'Universal Credit: welfare that works' (DWP, 2010c), a White Paper which described the new benefit. The Welfare Reform Act 2012 outlined the framework for Universal Credit, and The Universal Credit Regulations 2013 provided the detailed policy for this new benefit. Amendments to the Universal Credit legislation were passed in the Welfare Reform and Work Act 2016. Key changes included increasing the conditionality within Universal Credit by lowering the thresholds (the age of the youngest child) at which lead carers have to carry out work preparation and job search requirements.

The original timeframe for the implementation of Universal Credit was from 2013 to 2017. Following early problems, particularly with the new information technology system required for Universal Credit, the roll-out period was extended, and subsequently there have been several further delays to the roll-out schedule (Kennedy and Keen, 2018). The phased roll-out of Universal Credit began in April 2013 with simple cases in one site in the UK, and by the end of 2018, it was fully rolled out to all new claims in sites across the UK. Remaining benefit and tax credit claimants are expected to be transferred to Universal Credit by September 2024 (House of Commons Library, 2021). Some benefit and tax credit claimants will transition to Universal Credit earlier if they have a change of circumstances, such as losing a job or forming a couple relationship with a Universal Credit claimant (DWP, 2019a). Thus, despite setbacks, Universal Credit has become increasingly established.

Re-orientating the benefits system around paid work

The aims of Universal Credit are to simplify the benefits system, improve financial incentives to undertake paid work, reduce poverty, make the benefits system fairer and more affordable, and reduce error and fraud (DWP, 2010c, 2012b). The government has contended that the complexity and poor work incentives of the legacy system leads to worklessness and welfare dependency (DWP, 2010b, 2010c, 2014a, 2015a). In the Universal Credit literature, welfare dependency is portrayed as a sizable, growing and costly problem in the UK, and worklessness is presented as a generational problem affecting households and communities. The initial Universal Credit literature contains references to the need to reinforce 'pro-work social norms' (DWP, 2010c, p 59) and 'reintroduce the culture of work in households where it may have been absent for generations' (DWP, 2010c, p 3). The government claimed that worklessness and dependency result in unsustainable financial costs to the Exchequer and social costs to the country, and are a root cause of poverty (DWP, 2010a, 2010c). As such, the legacy system was perceived to maintain, rather than address, poverty by undermining paid work and facilitating poor choices and undesirable behaviour.

The government's solution to the perceived problems of the benefits system was to reorient it around paid work, as this was considered the best route out of poverty (DWP, 2010a, 2010c). The government argued that paid work is beneficial to physical and mental health, improves children's prospects and prevents perpetual generational worklessness (Work and Pensions Committee, 2015). Undertaking paid work has also been portrayed as necessary for full citizenship. The government explained that it wanted to 'create a welfare system that provides people with the confidence and security to play a full part in society through a flexible labour market within a competitive modern economy' (DWP, 2010c, p 12). Taking any paid work is perceived to be beneficial given the government's belief that this increases the likelihood of increasing earnings and securing employment (DWP, 2017b). Therefore, the introduction of Universal Credit is intended to increase moves into paid employment of any type and increase progression (in terms of the number of work hours and the pay levels) in the paid labour market (DWP, 2010b, 2010c, 2017b).

To increase entry and progression in paid work, Universal Credit policy aims to change attitudes and behaviours towards the benefits system and paid work (DWP, 2012b, 2016, 2017b; Sainsbury, 2014). Universal Credit is underpinned by a 'theory of change' (illustrated in Figure 3.1).[1] The government anticipates that changes in the benefits system (particularly increased incentives, simplification and intensified conditionality) will interact with individual circumstances and attitudes (and, where relevant, override these) to result in improved labour market outcomes (DWP, 2017b). By implementing Universal Credit, the government also aspires to move people from dependence on the state to independence regarding both paid work and the way claimants manage their finances (DWP, 2014a). Thus Universal Credit is intended to have far-reaching impacts on the views and actions of claimants.

There has been a mixed response to the rationale and aims of Universal Credit. The aims to improve financial incentives and simplify the benefits system have garnered

1 DEL/AME refers to Departmental Expenditure Limits/Annually Managed Expenditure; IT refers to information technology; JSA refers to Jobseekers' Allowance; UC refers to Universal Credit.

Figure 3.1: The Universal Credit theory of change

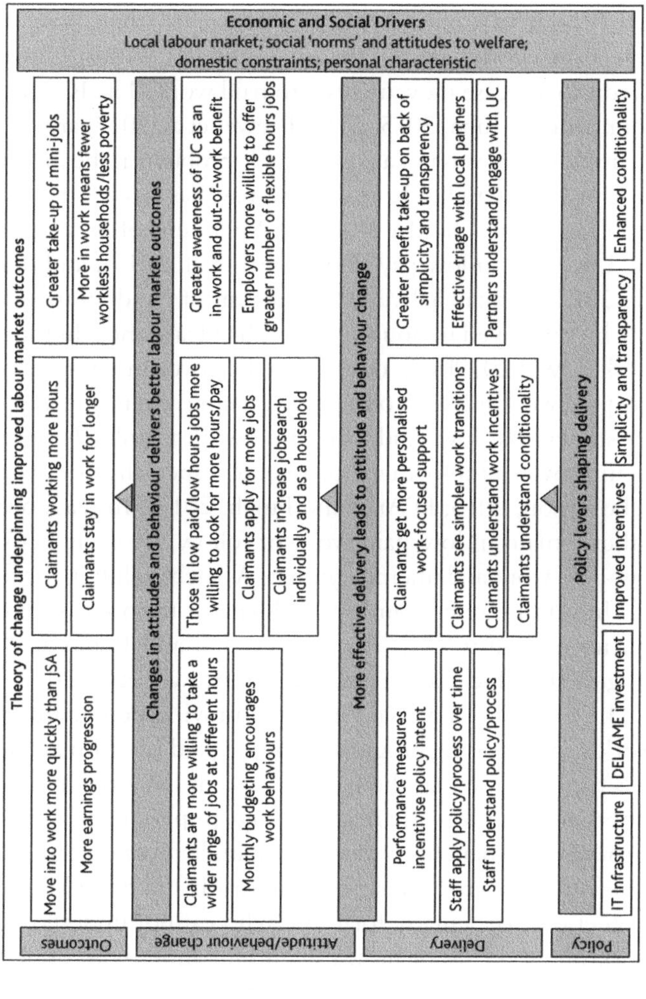

Source: DWP (2017b)

support from across the political spectrum (Sainsbury, 2014; Millar and Bennett, 2017; Work and Pensions Committee, 2017) and have in the main been commended (for example, Sainsbury, 2010; Citizens Advice, 2011; Finch, 2015; Work and Pensions Committee, 2017). However, there have been objections to the central priority inherent within Universal Credit to increase movements into paid work. The Resolution Foundation (Finch, 2015, 2016; Brewer et al, 2017) argues that unemployment was not a considerable problem at the inception of Universal Credit. Instead, low pay has been a persistent problem in the UK. In 2018, 17.2 per cent of employees in the UK were in low pay (Cominetti et al, 2019), and during the 2017/18 financial year, 69 per cent of children in relative low income lived in households with at least one adult in paid work (DWP, 2019b). In contrast to the government's view that any paid work is likely to improve earnings over time, research has shown that low-paid, part-time work is unlikely to result in improved employment prospects, especially for women (Thompson, 2015; D'Arcy and Finch, 2017). Instead, people either remain in low-paid work or follow the cycle between low-paid work and unemployment. As such, a shift in the focus of Universal Credit from unemployment to low pay and the quality of paid work is required (Veitch and Bennett, 2010; Judge, 2013; Field and Forsey, 2016; Brewer et al, 2017).

The focus in Universal Credit on moving people into paid work and increasing progression in the paid labour market also fails to recognise that the benefits system has a much broader scope and purpose than increasing employment rates and earnings. The benefits system has multiple functions, including preventing poverty, redistributing wealth and providing social protection, particularly for those who cannot undertake paid work due to crises or ill health and for those who undertake unpaid care of children and the elderly (Veitch and Bennett, 2010; Bennett, 2011; Millar, 2015). Therefore, the aspiration of Universal Credit to reorient the benefits system around paid work reflects an overly narrow conception of the social security system (Millar and Bennett, 2017). It marginalises those who cannot engage in paid work for legitimate reasons: for some in receipt of Universal Credit, undertaking paid work is not a possibility, and centring the social security system on paid work undermines the genuine entitlement they have to social protection. It also devalues other socially valid contributions, such as caring and volunteering (Veitch and Bennett, 2010; Richards-Gray, 2020). This ideology has very problematic financial outcomes: those who are not engaged in paid work for legitimate reasons will always be poorer than those who are in paid work. This may in effect penalise those who are disabled, have ill health or make essential societal contributions, such as undertaking unpaid care.

The contested aims and assumptions behind Universal Credit have influenced the design and delivery of this policy. The Universal Credit framework has been 'designed to produce positive behavioural effects' (DWP, 2010a, p 2) that move people off benefits and into paid work. The design is also intended to mimic paid work in order to help ease the transition into it (Work and Pensions Committee, 2017). This includes instituting a different relationship between claimants and the DWP wherein the DWP is portrayed as an employer who pays individuals for job search of up to 35 hours a week (Couling, 2016; Timmins, 2016). Thus, the design of Universal Credit is intended to both promote and replicate the world of paid work (Millar and Bennett, 2017). It attempts to achieve this and other aims of Universal Credit by making five key changes to the legacy system: increasing financial incentives to undertake paid work, simplifying the system, transferring responsibility for household budgeting to claimants, increasing conditionality and introducing online claims and account management.

Regarding the increase in conditionality under Universal Credit, the work-related requirements of the legacy regime have been intensified – for example, there is now a requirement of up to 35 hours of weekly job search. Additionally, conditionality has been expanded to include partners with children and those undertaking low-paid work (DWP, 2010c, 2011a). There have also been changes to paid work requirements of self-employed claimants. Following a one-year start-up period in which newly self-employed claimants are subject to certain work-related requirements, the minimum income floor (MIF) is applied. The MIF is the level of earnings the government expects an employed person to be earning in similar circumstances. The MIF is applied monthly, and if self-employed earnings are below the MIF, the claimant's payment is based on the MIF rather than actual earnings (DWP, 2020d). The implementation of Universal Credit also involves a more severe benefits sanctions regime. Table 3.1 illustrates the sanctions regime that was in operation during the course of the fieldwork (in November 2019, the duration of the highest-level sanctions was reduced to 182 days). Single parents and main carers of children in couples have been particular targets of the intensified and expanded conditionality within Universal Credit (DWP, 2010b). The new conditionality regime for lead carers is detailed after the following brief overview of the history of conditionality in the UK.

History of welfare conditionality in the UK

In the UK, access to employment benefits has always been conditional on involuntary employment, being available for paid work, actively seeking paid work and accepting job offers (Trickey and Walker, 2001; Griggs and Evans, 2010; Watts et al, 2014; Dwyer, 2016; Fletcher and Wright, 2018). However, the Conservative governments of 1979–97 intensified conditionality and expanded it to include specific paid work-related behavioural requirements (Trickey and Walker, 2001; Watts et al, 2014; Dwyer, 2016). Two key changes were made to the benefits system. The first was the introduction of the Restart programme in 1986, wherein unemployed claimants, after six months of receiving benefits, had to attend a Jobcentre appointment to demonstrate that they were actively seeking

Table 3.1: Universal Credit sanctions regime, 2013–19

Level of sanction	Length of sanction		
	First failure	Second failure within a year	Third failure within a year
High-level sanctions • Failing to undertake Mandatory Work Activity • Failing to apply for or to accept paid work • Ceasing paid work or losing pay for specified reasons	91 days	182 days	1,095 days
Medium-level sanctions • Failing to be available for paid work or to take all reasonable action to get paid work	28 days	91 days	91 days
Low-level sanctions • Failing to meet a work-focused interview requirement • Failing to comply with a work-related requirement • Failing to meet a work preparation requirement • Failing to take a particular action to get paid work	Until claimant complies plus 7 days	Until claimant complies plus 14 days	Until claimant complies plus 28 days
Lowest-level sanctions • Failing to meet a work-focused interview requirement	Until claimant complies	Until claimant complies	Until claimant complies

Source: Adapted from Kennedy and Keen (2016)

work. Nonattendance could result in a sanction (Dwyer and Ellison, 2009a). The second key change was the introduction of Jobseeker's Allowance (JSA) in 1996, which is viewed as a watershed moment in the history of the UK benefits system (Freedland and King, 2003; Watts et al, 2014; Fletcher and

Wright, 2018). Under this policy, claimants had to attend fortnightly interviews at the Jobcentre and sign a Jobseeker's Agreement. This stipulated their availability for paid work and the specific job search activities they were required to carry out under threat of sanction (Trickey and Walker, 2001; Griggs et al, 2014).

The Conservative governments' changes to the benefits system laid the foundation for the reforms of the New Labour government (1997–2010) (Trickey and Walker, 2001; Griggs et al, 2014; Fletcher and Wright, 2018). Conditionality was central to these reforms (Dwyer, 2016) and was significantly intensified and expanded by the introduction of a series of New Deals (Dwyer and Ellison, 2009a). Initially, the New Deal for Young People was implemented; this mandated participation in one of four paid work and training options, with sanctions for failure to participate ranging between 2 and 26 weeks (Dwyer and Ellison, 2009a; Griggs et al, 2014). Other New Deals with varying requirements and degrees of compulsion were also implemented, resulting in the extension of conditionality to groups previously exempt from work-related expectations, such as single parents, disabled people and partners of unemployed claimants (Trickey and Walker, 2001; Griggs et al, 2014). The policies of the subsequent Conservative–Liberal Democrat Coalition government and then the Conservative governments have further intensified the approach to conditionality adopted by New Labour (Dwyer, 2016), as evidenced in the introduction of Universal Credit, which entails the most extensive and intensive application of conditionality to date (Dwyer and Wright, 2014; Wright and Dwyer, 2022).

The implementation of conditionality in the UK has been underpinned by belief in an 'underclass' of welfare dependents, who are not sufficiently motivated to undertake paid work and prefer to receive their income from social security benefits, and who pass on this perceived culture of worklessness to subsequent generations (Macdonald et al,

2014). Regarding Universal Credit specifically, government rhetoric has followed the 'underclass' discourse of 1980s conservative thought (Kowalewska, 2015). This has been used to justify both the introduction of Universal Credit and the expansion of conditionality (DWP, 2010b, 2010c, 2014a, 2015a). The implementation of conditionality in the UK is also underpinned by other assumptions, such as the primacy of paid work as the central citizenship obligation. This is evident too in the Universal Credit literature (DWP, 2010c). As UK governments have considered that the problems of poverty and unemployment are caused by the behaviour of benefits recipients and that paid work is 'the best form of welfare' (DWP, 2008, p 25), they have implemented conditionality, an essentially behaviouristic policy (Whitworth and Griggs, 2013; Etherington and Daguerre, 2015), to get claimants into paid work. As Deacon explains, 'The primary purpose of such welfare conditionality is not to determine entitlement or to establish need, but to change behaviour' (2004, p 912). This emphasis on behaviour change is apparent in the Universal Credit theory of change, previously discussed.

There are considerable objections to the implementation of conditionality in the UK. A key objection is that it erodes the social rights Marshall extolled (King, 1999; Dwyer, 2004, 2016). Marshall defined social rights as 'the whole range from the right to a modicum of economic welfare and security to the right to share to the full in the social heritage and to live the life of a civilised being according to the standards prevailing in society' (1950, p 8). As this shows, Marshall viewed that social citizenship entails at the very least the right to basic financial provision. Marshall's consideration of responsibilities was brief: instead his emphasis was on rights, which he viewed as universal and largely unconditional (Dwyer, 2000, 2004, 2016; Etherington and Daguerre, 2015). However, through implementing conditionality, successive governments have reformulated rights and responsibilities (Paz-Fuchs, 2008; Dwyer and Wright, 2014; Reeves and Loopstra, 2017).

Responsibilities have been emphasised over rights (King, 1999; Lister, 2011; Dwyer, 2016), with undertaking paid work being the predominant responsibility (Wright, 2011; Griggs et al, 2014; Dwyer, 2016). Eligibility to access social rights is now contingent on paid work-related behaviour rather than entitlement and need (Dwyer, 2004). This is contested as it fundamentally undermines the status of social rights (King, 1999; Dean, 2001; Dwyer, 2004, 2016; Paz-Fuchs, 2008). People can no longer be guaranteed access to the resources necessary to meet basic needs if this can be denied on the basis of state-stipulated behaviour. The challenge to social citizenship rights posed by the implementation of conditionality is particularly problematic given that the reduction of social rights and increase in responsibilities has mainly affected poor people (Dwyer, 1998, 2004; Lister, 2011). Consequently, the poorest and most vulnerable members of society are most likely to be negatively impacted by the implementation of conditionality (Dwyer, 2004; Grover, 2012).

The empirical research carried out to date provides little support for claims that conditionality is effective in sustainably improving employment rates and incomes. Findings from the Welfare Conditionality Project (Dwyer, 2018b) along with other studies investigating the impact of conditionality on specific groups, including single parents (Goodwin, 2008) and disabled people (Reeves, 2017), have found that conditionality is of little efficacy in improving moves into employment. Two reviews of the international evidence (Griggs and Evans, 2010; National Audit Office, 2016) conclude that benefits sanctions increase both exits from benefits and employment rates; however, there are negative impacts on earnings over time, and the effects on employment can be short-lived. Quantitative research from the UK (Loopstra et al, 2015) found that while sanctions increase exits from unemployment benefits, only 20 per cent of claimants move into paid work, while the other 80 per cent move into destinations unrelated to paid work. There is also evidence which shows that sanction-backed conditionality results in lower earnings over time and less secure employment, and that claimants accept jobs at a lower occupational level (Arni et al, 2013; van den Berg and Vikström, 2014). Although there was already research showing that conditionality is of limited efficacy, including in relation to single parents (Goodwin, 2008; Johnsen and Blenkinsopp, 2018), prior to the fieldwork discussed in this book, there was an absence of research investigating conditionality from a gender perspective. This added to the impetus to carry out research investigating the gendered impacts of the Universal Credit conditionality regime.

Universal Credit conditionality regime for lead carers

Before the introduction of Universal Credit, single and coupled mothers in the UK were under different conditionality regimes. Previously, main carers of children in couples were subject to minimal work-related requirements, whereas single parents were particular targets of increased conditionality (Wright, 2011; Whitworth and Griggs, 2013). During New Labour's time in office, main carers of children in couples were not required to seek paid work. Main carers of children were labelled as the 'dependent partner' of the main claimant, and work-related requirements were limited to work-focused interviews, introduced from 2004. Partners of Employment and Support Allowance recipients and Income Support recipients were required to attend a single work-focused interview. Partners of JSA recipients were mandated to attend one work-focused interview every six months, under the threat of sanction for noncompliance (Dorsett et al, 2006; DWP, 2011b).

At the beginning of New Labour's time in office, single parents in the UK were subject to a light conditionality regime in comparison with other OECD countries: single parents were not required to look for paid work until their youngest child left school at the age of either 16 or 18 years (Haux, 2012; Johnsen, 2014). Under the social security reforms of New Labour, conditionality for single parents increased incrementally. A key change was made in 2008 when single parents with a youngest child aged 12 years or above became ineligible for Income Support and had to claim JSA instead (Wright, 2011). The age threshold was subsequently lowered to 10 years in 2009 and 7 years in 2010. As recipients of JSA, single parents were treated similarly to other JSA claimants and were required to sign on every fortnight and be available for, and actively seek, paid work (Haux, 2012; Johnsen, 2014). Claimants had to carry out a certain number of specific job search steps each week, such as preparing a CV or contacting potential employers (Petrongolo, 2009; Kennedy, 2010). In an attempt to recognise the impact caring responsibilities can have on single parents' ability to seek and be available for paid work, 'single-parent flexibilities' were incorporated into the JSA regulations in 2008.

Through the implementation of Universal Credit, conditionality has been intensified for single parents and mandatory job search and preparation requirements have been extended to the main carer of children in couples. In order to receive Universal Credit, claimants are required to accept an individual Claimant Commitment (DWP, 2020b). The Claimant Commitment details the claimant's specific work-related requirements, including the mandated hours of job search and preparation, the claimant's availability for paid work and the time they need to travel to look for paid work. It also stipulates the sanctions that may be issued for noncompliance with work-related requirements. The Claimant Commitment is drawn up with the claimant's Jobcentre Plus (JCP) work coach as part of the claiming process, but it can be subsequently reviewed and updated (DWP, 2020b). Couples must make a joint claim, and both members of the couple need to accept their separate Claimant Commitments before they can receive Universal Credit payments. If one member of the couple receives a sanction, the couple's standard allowance is reduced by up to 50 per cent (DWP, 2020a).

Under Universal Credit, couples with children are required to nominate one member of the couple as the lead carer, and single parents are automatically designated the lead carer. Lead carers are subject to different levels of work-related requirements depending on the age of the youngest child, as shown in Table 3.2. Work coaches have discretion in setting

Table 3.2: Work-related requirements for lead carers

Age of your youngest child	Your responsibilities
Under 1	You do not need to look for work in order to receive Universal Credit.
Age 1	If you are not already working, you do not need to look for work in order to receive Universal Credit. You will be asked to attend work-focused interviews with your work coach to discuss plans for a future move into work and will need to report any changes of circumstances.
Age 2	You will be expected to take active steps to prepare for work. This will involve having regular work-focused interviews with your work coach, agreeing a programme of activities tailored to your individual circumstances which might include some training and work preparation activities (for example, writing your CV).
Age 3 or 4	You will be expected to work a maximum of 16 hours a week (or spend 16 hours a week looking for work). This might include some training and work-focused interviews.
Age between 5 and 12	You will be expected to work a maximum of 25 hours a week (or spend 25 hours a week looking for work). This might include some training and work-focused interviews.
Age 13 and above	You will be expected to work a maximum of 35 hours a week (or spend 35 hours a week looking for work). This might include some training and work-focused interviews.

Source: DWP (2020e)

these work-related requirements. The government literature regarding lead carers states that the type and location of paid work and the number of hours claimants need to be available for paid work will be tailored to their individual circumstances and caring responsibilities (DWP, 2015c, 2020e). The government also states that requirements for job search may be reduced if there is a lack of free and affordable childcare accessible to the claimant (DWP, 2020e). Additionally, easements involving the reduction or removal of work-related requirements due to personal circumstances – including domestic abuse, ill health, housing situation and temporary childcare requirements – can be applied (DWP, 2020a). Some easements are a legal requirement – for example, in the case of domestic abuse; some are at the discretion of the work coach – for example, in the case of temporary childcare requirements (DWP, 2018b).

Under Universal Credit, conditionality is applied to claimants whose earnings are below the Conditionality Earnings Threshold (CET) (DWP, 2017a). The CET is calculated by multiplying the number of hours the claimant is expected to undertake paid work by the National Minimum Wage and then converting this figure to a monthly amount. Therefore, unemployed single parents are subject to conditionality and single parents in paid work can be subject to in-work conditionality (and potentially required to seek more hours, higher wages or a second job) if their earnings are below the CET applicable to them. Unemployed lead carers in couples are subject to conditionality if the other member of the couple is unemployed or their monthly earnings are below the sum of their individual thresholds (the household CET). Due to the presence of both the individual CET and the household CET, the policy regarding in-work conditionality for couples is more complex (SSAC, 2017). Lead carers can be subject to in-work conditionality in a variety of scenarios. For example, if the household earnings are below the household CET and the main earner is working full-time at the minimum wage, the lead carer can be subject to in-work conditionality if their earnings are below their individual CET. Consequently, the earnings of one partner affects the work-related requirements of the other, and if one partner's engagement in paid work changes, this may alter the requirements of the other partner (DWP, 2020a).

The level of individual or household earnings also determines the intensity of conditionality that claimants are subject to. In addition to the CET, there is the Administrative Earnings Threshold (AET), which is a fixed amount.[2] Claimants earning below the AET are subject to intensive work-related conditions, including job search (SSAC, 2017). Single-parent claimants earning between the AET and the CET are subject to a less-intense conditionality regime, termed 'light touch',[3] and cannot be subject to job search or work availability requirements (SSAC, 2017; DWP, 2018a). For coupled lead carers, household income is taken into account. For example, a coupled lead carer who is not undertaking paid work can be subject to the light-touch regime if their partner is earning more than £541 per month but less than the Household CET. Consequently, Universal Credit particularly intensifies and expands conditionality to those who are unemployed or on the lowest of earnings.

The implementation of Universal Credit has also intensified conditionality for single parents through the changes made to single-parent flexibilities. The majority of the flexibilities have been downgraded to guidance and, therefore, do not have the authority of the law: their application is at the discretion of the individual's work coach (Cain, 2016). Flexibilities not taken into account in Universal Credit legislation include safeguards against the use of sanctions if single parents are unable to take up a job offer or have to leave a job due to lack of suitable

2 At the time of the fieldwork, the AET was £338 per month for single claimants and £541 for couples (Work and Pensions Committee, 2018a).

3 At the time of the fieldwork, the specific policy for the light-touch regime was yet to be finalised (Work and Pensions Committee, 2018a).

childcare (Gingerbread, 2013). Also, those with children aged 13 or older can only restrict their paid work hours according to their caring responsibilities if they can demonstrate that they have reasonable prospects of obtaining paid work within those reduced hours (Gingerbread, 2013).

Alongside the intensification of conditionality under Universal Credit, there has been an increase in state assistance with formal childcare provision. Universal Credit claimants can claim back up to 85 per cent of their childcare costs (DWP, 2020e), which is an increase from the 70 per cent provided under Working Tax Credit. This amount is capped at £646 for one child and £1,108 for two or more children per month (DWP, 2020e). Childcare provision has also been expanded under Universal Credit through extending help with childcare costs to parents working less than 16 hours per week (DWP, 2014b). In addition, some parents of 3- and 4-year-olds in the general UK population are eligible for up to 30 hours per week (for 38 weeks per year) of state-funded formal childcare (HMG, 2018). For eligible parents, this is an increase from the 15 hours per week available to all 3- and 4-year-olds.

As demonstrated, the introduction of the conditionality regime for lead carers within Universal Credit has expanded and intensified the mandatory work-related requirements of main carers of children. The implementation of Universal Credit extends work preparation and job search requirements to coupled main carers of children for the first time. Universal Credit policy also intensifies conditionality for single parents through lowering the threshold (the age of the youngest child) at which they are expected to prepare for and look for paid work, and increasing job search requirements from a prescribed number of job search activities to a mandated number of job search hours (which can be up to 35 per week). Conditionality for single parents has also been intensified under Universal Credit through the implementation of a more severe sanctions regime, the erosion of single-parent flexibilities and the introduction of conditionality for those in paid work. The changes in conditionality under Universal Credit also extend conditionality to both coupled and single mothers unaffected under the previous system, such as those in receipt of Housing Benefit and tax credits (which did not have any work-related conditions attached).

Gender concerns

Prior to the full roll-out of Universal Credit, gender concerns were raised about the new conditionality regime that are pertinent to the gendered social security system and women's citizenship. Concerns were raised that the conditionality within Universal Credit devalues unpaid care (Deacon and Patrick, 2011; Whitworth and Griggs, 2013; Davies, 2015; Cain, 2016). Particular elements of the Universal Credit conditionality regime were highlighted, such as the threshold at which mandatory job search conditions apply to lead carers. When the Welfare Reform and Work Bill was introduced in 2015, objections were raised to proposals to subject lead carers with a youngest child aged 3 or 4 years old to job search requirements (CPAG, 2015a, 2015b; Gingerbread, 2015; House of Lords Hansard, 2015a). These objections were made on the grounds that parental care and contact in the early years are particularly critical – for example, in terms of child development and outcomes in later life – and that unpaid care is important work. The extensiveness of the required job search hours and paid work hours within Universal Credit were also criticised for their potential to limit the time and energy mothers have to carry out unpaid care (House of Lords Hansard, 2015b).

Concerns were also raised that the designation of lead carers within Universal Credit would have implications for women's position in the paid labour market. The government has stated that due to the new conditionality regime, Universal Credit 'presents an opportunity to promote equality in work and narrow the employment gap' (DWP, 2012c, p 42). However, charities highlighted the problematic combination of women's predominance in low-paid, insecure work and the emphasis in Universal Credit on moving people into work at the first opportunity rather than focusing on helping claimants obtain high-quality, sustainable work (Fawcett Society, 2015; Gingerbread, 2015). Under Universal Credit, the government is explicitly trying to move claimants into any type of work, including temporary and part-time jobs they may not have previously considered (DWP, 2017b). This constitutes a 'work first' approach, entailing moving claimants into any type of work as quickly as possible, and has been criticised for encouraging claimants into obtaining low-paid and inappropriate jobs (Lindsay et al, 2007). Therefore, there were concerns that the conditionality would cement existing gender inequalities in the paid labour market, particularly for low-income mothers.

Claims were also made that the conditionality within Universal Credit has the potential to deny mothers the choice to undertake unpaid care and to restrict their agency in regard to decisions about their engagement in the paid labour market (Davies, 2012, 2015; Whitworth and Griggs, 2013; Rafferty and Wiggan, 2017; Millar, 2019). Charities criticised the lowering of the threshold for job search to when the youngest child is aged 3 on the grounds that this denies parents' choice regarding engagement in unpaid care and paid work in the crucial early years of their children's development (CPAG, 2015b; Gingerbread, 2015). Regarding older children, it has been argued that parents are best placed to know the appropriate level of engagement in unpaid care and paid work and, as such, should be able to determine this for themselves (Judge, 2015). The application of in-work conditionality to single parents was criticised on similar grounds. There were concerns that in-work conditionality could result in mandatory expectations of paid work hours that conflict with parental choices regarding engagement in unpaid care and paid work (Rafferty and Wiggan, 2017).

There was an element of uncertainty as to whether the gender concerns would be realised in the lives of women subject to the new conditionality regime within Universal Credit. This was in part due to the increased discretion afforded to work coaches, who are responsible for setting work-related requirements (including the mandatory hours of job search, the type of work claimants are mandated to seek and the geographical location of job search), tailoring work-related requirements to lead carers' caring responsibilities (DWP, 2015c) and giving claimants employment-related support (DWP, 2015a). Also, under Universal Credit, work coaches can direct claimants to apply for specific jobs, with the potential for sanctions as a consequence of noncompliance (DWP, 2018a). Therefore, it was important to explore the role of the work coach as part of investigating whether the gender concerns were realised in the lives of women subject to the new conditionality regime.

Conclusion

The introduction of Universal Credit is intended to reorient the benefits system around paid work, and one key means of achieving this – the intensification and expansion of conditionality – may have particular implications for women. Universal Credit introduces a new conditionality regime for lead carers of children which intensifies conditionality for single parents and extends job search requirements to coupled parents for the first time. Due to their disproportionate responsibility for unpaid care, women are more likely to be subject to the new conditionality regime for lead carers of children. Concerns have been raised that the conditionality for lead carers within Universal Credit may devalue unpaid care, exacerbate women's disadvantaged position in the paid labour market and limit women's agency. Single mothers may particularly be subject to conditionality given that coupled mothers can be exempt (or subject to less stringent requirements) if their partner's earnings are above a particular level. However, coupled mothers may face financial loss due to the actions of their partner, because if one partner receives a sanction, the whole family is likely to be impacted as there is one monthly payment into one account (Millar and Bennett, 2017).

These concerns warranted investigation, particularly given the historical and continuing devaluation of unpaid care, women's ongoing weaker labour market position and the myriad constraints that are already placed on women's agency in relation to their engagement in paid work and unpaid care (see Chapter Two). Additionally, at the time of the fieldwork, the academic research and literature concerning Universal Credit and gender mainly focused on the financial elements of this new benefit (Bennett, 2012; Bennett and Sung, 2013a, 2013b, 2014), and there was a lack of empirical research concerning the potential gendered implications of conditionality for lead carers within Universal Credit. The next three chapters present the research findings and show the extent to which, and ways in which, the gender concerns are realised in the lives of women subject to the Universal Credit conditionality regime.

FOUR

Universal Credit and unpaid care: "we're doing a massive job anyway"

Introduction

Women have a marginalised position in the UK social security system. This ongoing disadvantaged position is related to the dominant gendered concept of citizenship, which is based around masculine activities, attributes and interactions with the paid labour market. To create a more inclusive citizenship framework, some feminists have argued that citizenship needs to be redefined to recognise the importance of unpaid care (Knijn and Kremer, 1997; Sevenhuijsen, 2000; Tronto, 2001; Pateman, 2005). This would entail the implementation of social security policies that support parents financially so they can carry out unpaid care (Pateman, 2005; Gillies, 2007; Lynch and Walsh, 2009). However, in the UK and beyond, there has been an increasing application of conditionality, which may work against feminist aims to create citizenship frameworks that promote unpaid care as a valid societal contribution (see Chapter Two). To investigate concerns that the conditionality within Universal Credit fails to recognise and value unpaid care (Deacon and Patrick, 2011; Whitworth and Griggs, 2013; Davies, 2015; Cain, 2016), this chapter explores how, and why, the conditionality for lead carers within Universal Credit affects women's roles and responsibilities regarding unpaid care over time. The chapter begins by outlining the participants' caring responsibilities. It continues by discussing the extent to which caring responsibilities were taken into account during the Universal Credit claim. It then explores the effects of the conditionality within Universal Credit on the mothers' caring responsibilities. The final section discusses the mothers' commitment to unpaid care and their views on whether unpaid care is valued within the Universal Credit system.

Overview of the participants' caring responsibilities

Women remain disproportionately responsible for unpaid care despite their entrance in significant numbers into the paid labour market (Lewis, 2009; Orloff, 2009; Boyer et al, 2017; Jupp et al, 2019). The gendered imbalance in responsibility for unpaid care was strongly evident across the sample. At the first wave of interviews, the fathers had regular contact time with their children in only 5 of the 21 single-parent families. For the rest of the single-parent families, there was either no contact time at all or irregular contact between the fathers and children. In some cases, contact with the father was not possible – for example, due to previous domestic abuse (experienced by six of the mothers) or because the father lived far away. Some of the mothers explained how the lack of contact their children had with their fathers impacted their caring responsibilities:

> 'Given also, like, their dad's behaviour, and he's not really involved, I kind of really want to be there for them … we don't have any other relatives here and we're not really in touch with my husband's family. … I am all they have, so I need to be there for them.' (Jennifer,[1] single mother, two children aged 6 and 3, wave one)

1 Pseudonyms have been used throughout this book to preserve the anonymity of the participants.

> 'They don't see their dads really, so I'm like mum and dad.' (Angela, single mother, two children aged 8 and 5, wave one)

Of the three coupled families, in one couple the mother and father carried out a fairly equal amount of the unpaid care, in another the mother carried out the majority of the unpaid care, and in the other, the child spent half of his time with his mother and her new partner and half with his father.

Regarding help with childcare from family and friends, two of the mothers had regular help and one of the mothers had various family members who were available to help as and when needed. Many of the mothers had either occasional help or help available in an emergency. Five of the mothers had no help from family and friends. In addition, in ten of the families, one or more of the children had additional needs (in the form of speech delays, learning disabilities or mental health issues) or needed extra support following their parents' separation or divorce. Overall, the majority of the mothers interviewed had either the sole or the vast majority of the responsibility for the care of the children, with little support from family and friends. This gendered imbalance in responsibility for unpaid care was significant to the mothers' experiences of conditionality and was rarely recognised within the Universal Credit system, as discussed next.

Extent to which caring responsibilities were taken into account

The formation of the Claimant Commitment, which stipulates work-related requirements, is of crucial importance in the recognition of caring responsibilities. According to government literature, work coaches tailor work-related requirements (including the type of work, location of work and hours claimants need to be available for work) to individual circumstances (including caring responsibilities) (DWP, 2020e). Ongoing interactions with work coaches are also relevant to the extent to which caring responsibilities are taken into account, as work coaches are largely responsible for implementing conditionality on an ongoing basis. For example, after an initial period, work coaches can determine the frequency, length and format (for example, in person or by telephone) of work search review appointments (SSAC, 2019). This section considers the limited extent to which caring responsibilities were taken into account when the Claimant Commitment was formed and during ongoing interactions with work coaches, and discusses the extensiveness of the work-related requirements.

Forming the Claimant Commitment

In contrast to the government literature (DWP, 2020e), the majority of the mothers interviewed did not think their caring responsibilities were taken into account when the work-related requirements were set. Most of the mothers felt that there was a singular emphasis on paid work and that it was their responsibility to negotiate the work-related requirements of Universal Credit and their caring responsibilities:

> 'They didn't really talk about that. It felt like that was just my responsibility, whatever I did. Like, I'm being helped with X amount of money and I've got to divide that up and figure out how I'm going to look after my kids on my own.' (Louise, single mother, two children aged 8 and 6, wave one)

> 'They don't ask you nothing. And I don't even think they really care … kids don't come into consideration. Being [a] single parent doesn't come into consideration at all. Cos they're talking about jobs.' (Leanne, single mother, three children aged 12, 10 and 5, wave one)

Many of the other participants also said they were not asked about their caring responsibilities – for example whether their children had any contact time with their fathers or whether they had any help with childcare from family or friends. The absence of discussions regarding caring responsibilities is significant, particularly for those with extensive responsibilities, as this is a necessary precursor to tailoring work-related requirements. 'Michelle', a single mother whose children only saw their father every other weekend and who did not have family or friends to help with childcare, expressed resentment at the lack of discussion of her personal circumstances and the setting of the standard expectation of 25 hours of job search:

> 'On what basis have you [work coach] decided that I have a spare 25 hours a week to give to you or to work with two children? He doesn't understand any of my personal circumstances so how can he make that assumption that I can do that?' (Michelle, single mother, two children aged 10 and 7, wave two)

Six of the mothers did perceive that their caring responsibilities were taken into account when their work-related requirements were set. 'Kirsty' said her work coach

> 'was very understanding and she made sure that when we was discussing Commitments, my children was kind of taken into consideration.' (Kirsty, single mother, two children aged 7 and 5, wave one)

Kirsty's work coach set her weekly hours of job search at 20 hours, rather than the standard 25 hours applicable given her youngest child's age. This was because when Kirsty first claimed Universal Credit, she had recently been served an eviction notice. Similarly, four of the other five mothers who thought their caring responsibilities had been taken into account had an easement in their work-related requirements (on the grounds of health, their housing situation or experiences of domestic abuse). Most of these easements are a legal requirement (see Chapter Three). Only one mother who did not have an easement reported that her work coach took her caring responsibilities into account. This mother explained that her work coach was understanding and tailored the distance the participant was required to travel to look for paid work. Some of the other mothers similarly received a reduction in the distance that they were required to travel to find paid work on account of their caring responsibilities, and in this regard there was some recognition of caring responsibilities. However, none of the mothers received a reduction in their job search hours – an arguably more salient aspect of the Claimant Commitment – on account of their caring responsibilities.

The limited extent to which caring responsibilities were taken into account in the participants' Claimant Commitments corresponds with findings from the Welfare Conditionality Project (Johnsen and Blenkinsopp, 2018). Research investigating the tailoring of Claimant Commitments to personal circumstances within the broader population of claimants has found inconsistencies (SSAC, 2019), and a public inquiry into benefits sanctions found that for many groups of claimants, including single parents, Claimant Commitments are not personalised (Work and Pensions Committee, 2018a).

Ongoing interactions with work coaches

The participants' ongoing interactions with their work coaches also give indications of the limited extent to which caring responsibilities are recognised within the Universal Credit conditionality regime. The study highlighted two relevant issues: the arrangements for work search review appointments and job search requirements during school holidays. Regarding work search review appointments, several mothers spoke of appointments being arranged for times that were not compatible with caring responsibilities – for example, outside school hours or during school drop-off and pick-up times. As 'Leanne', a single mother who was in paid work and subject to in-work conditionality, explained of her phone appointments:

> 'They're making the phone calls at quarter past three. Well I'm at the school gate at quarter past three. You miss that appointment, you get sanctioned.' (Leanne, single mother, three children aged thirteen, 10 and 5, wave two)

Other participants expressed frustration at the lack of consideration of caring responsibilities when work search review appointments were arranged. However, consistent with the earlier finding that the mothers with easements tended to think their caring responsibilities had been taken into account when the Claimant Commitments were formed, some of the mothers with easements reported that their work coaches demonstrated consideration of caring responsibilities when making arrangements for appointments:

> 'The work coach was understanding because actually she'd make the appointments in school time. So she'd go, "Oh no, it's three o'clock – we can't do the three o'clock one because you'll have your son coming home".' (Helen, single mother, two children aged 13 and 11, wave two)

This demonstrates the importance of work coaches who have a detailed awareness of the responsibilities involved in caring for children (House of Lords Hansard, 2015a).

While the work coaches' consideration of caring responsibilities was variable in regard to setting appointment times, there was a uniform lack of consideration of caring responsibilities with respect to job search requirements during school holidays. None of the mothers reported a reduction in job search requirements during the school holidays, and most stated that there was no discussion with their work coaches concerning this. When asked whether her work coach had discussed work-related requirements during the school holidays, 'Zoe' responded by saying:

> 'Oh no, no, no, no, because if you're at home, you're at home, you're not actually doing anything. … So you don't have to do any washing up or the washing or hoovering or cleaning or entertaining a child who's bored of being stuck in. Yeah, they don't, they don't consider that.' (Zoe, single mother, two children aged 14 and 7, wave two)

This lack of reduction in job search requirements during the school holidays is particularly problematic given that those searching for paid work are not eligible for help with childcare costs under Universal Credit (DWP, 2020c), and subsequently the mothers had to fulfil extensive work-related requirements while looking after their children full time (discussed further in Chapter Five). Previously, under the single-parent flexibilities (see Chapter Three), single parents were exempt from job search during the school holidays if it would be unreasonable for the claimant to arrange childcare. The absence of discussions around childcare in the school holidays and the lack of reductions in job search requirements suggests that the single-parent flexibilities are not being applied by work coaches. This reinforces concerns about the downgrading of these flexibilities from legislation to discretionary guidance under Universal Credit legislation (Gingerbread, 2013; Cain, 2016).

On the whole, the experiences and views of the mothers demonstrate that throughout the Universal Credit claim, work-related requirements are not tailored to claimants' caring responsibilities. One reason for this may be that work coaches are constrained by lack of time and high caseloads (Lipsky, 2010). Research conducted by the Social Security Advisory Committee (2019) suggests the lack of tailoring of Claimant Commitments is partly due to the brevity of the initial meeting, where this document is developed. Also, under

Universal Credit, work coaches have larger caseloads due to the increased number of people subject to conditionality and the reductions in contracted-out provision[2] (Work and Pensions Committee, 2016). Another reason for the lack of personalisation may be that the work coaches do not have the personal resources to tailor work-related requirements to caring responsibilities (Lipsky, 2010; Toerien et al, 2013). Under Universal Credit, work coaches are generalists who work with a range of claimants with different needs (Work and Pensions Committee, 2018a; SSAC, 2019). Since 2011, there has been a phasing out of specialist single-parent advisers (introduced by the New Labour government) at the JCP (Gingerbread, 2013; Fawcett Society, 2015). This may be particularly problematic for claimants with caring responsibilities. Previous research has indicated that the phasing out of these specialist advisors has led to a loss of understanding of the issues single parents face (Graham and McQuaid, 2014). As work coaches within Universal Credit are generalists, they may not have an awareness of pertinent issues – such as school drop-off and pick-up times, the challenges of trying to fulfil work-related requirements during school holidays or the relevance of the amount of contact time children have with their father – to a mother's ability to engage in paid work.

The extensiveness of work-related requirements

The absence of tailoring the standard work-related expectations to claimants' caring responsibilities is problematic given the extensiveness of the standard expectations stipulated in the Universal Credit legislation. At the first round of interviews,

2 In 2017, the Work Programme, wherein welfare-to-work provision was outsourced to private and third-party organisations, was ended and replaced by the Work and Health Programme. This new programme is much smaller in its scope, and therefore many claimants who previously would have been referred to external providers are now assigned to JCP work coaches.

Michelle was working 16 to 20 hours a week as a self-employed cleaner. She described her response to being told during a work search review appointment that she was expected to undertake paid work for 25 hours a week:

> 'I said, "I don't know how you expect that from a single mum". I said, 'I can't do it".' (Michelle, single mother, two children aged 9 and 7, wave one)

From Michelle's perspective, the standard work-related expectations are too high for single mothers, regardless of their circumstances. Many of the other mothers also thought the work-related requirements placed on them were too extensive and did not take into consideration the intensity of labour and the time involved in caring for children (Lynch and Walsh, 2009):

> 'shopping, cooking, cleaning, organising, planning diaries, thinking about managing behaviour, social life for children, managing money, budgeting … there's an awful lot that goes into managing a home and that you can't just necessarily guarantee that every single moment they're at school can be spent purely working.' (Lucy, single mother, two children aged 8 and 6, wave one)

This lack of recognition of caring responsibilities shows the dominance within Universal Credit of paid work over other forms of social contribution and demonstrates that women's unequal responsibility for unpaid care has been largely overlooked in conditionality policies (Wright, 2011; Ingold and Etherington, 2013). This was particularly problematic for the study's participants given the magnitude of their caring responsibilities. While there is some acknowledgement of caring responsibilities within the Universal Credit conditionality regime through the lower hours of required job search for lead carers of children aged 3 and 4, and 5 to 12 (16 and 25 hours, respectively), the expectations were still too high

for many participants. Unrealistic work-related expectations that were not eased by work coach discretion resulted in the participants being subject to work-related requirements that were incompatible with their caring responsibilities. This negatively impacted their caring responsibilities, discussed next.

Effects of work-related requirements and paid work on caring responsibilities

Concerns have been raised that conditionality policies fail to recognise that work-related requirements and paid employment can limit time and energy for fulfilling caring obligations (Pateman, 2005; Wright, 2011; Davies, 2012). The study's findings demonstrate the ways in which these concerns are realised in the lives of mothers subject to the conditionality within Universal Credit. This section discusses how work-related requirements and paid work affected the participants' time and interactions with their children, and highlights the challenges of taking children to the JCP.

Effects on time and interactions

During the course of the longitudinal research, the majority of participants referred to the negative impacts of work-related requirements and paid work on their caring responsibilities. For many of the mothers, the work-related requirements and paid work either reduced the amount of time spent with their children or meant that while they were with their children, they were carrying out their mandatory work-related requirements:

> 'I don't feel that I'm doing the best that I can as a mother to hand my children over to somebody else to look after them all day while I go out and work as many hours as I can, which is what is expected of us from Universal Credits.' (Christina, coupled mother, two children aged 15 and 6, wave one)

> 'There were times when, you know, [youngest child] wanted mummy to play or do whatever and I was, "No, I've just got to do this. I've got a meeting tomorrow. I need to do this." Or there were times when he was ill and I was taken away from the job search and I'm like in his bedroom, "Right, okay, I'll be …" and I'll be sneaking off.' (Jessica, single mother, two children aged 6 and 4, wave one)

The reduction in time spent with children had implications for the amount of involvement the mothers could have in their children's education and the support they could give them. Since claiming Universal Credit, 'Angela' obtained a job that entailed evening shifts. Subsequently, she was unable to continue to help her son (who had dyslexia) with his reading:

> 'He has got that difficulty as well, which is why I wanted to be more at home so that I could help him more, but I don't have the time now cos I'm at work on a night.' (Angela, single mother, two children aged 8 and 5, wave one)

The work-related requirements and paid work also reduced the time some of the mothers' had for carrying out household tasks involved in caring for children, such as cooking, tidying and cleaning. The limitations that engagement in work-related requirements and paid work placed on the mothers' ability to spend time with their children, support them educationally and carry out other tasks involved in caring for children may have been particularly difficult for the participants given current expectations of intensive mothering (Holloway and Pimlott-Wilson, 2016; Vincent, 2017). Michelle objected to the potential sanctions for not undertaking the required number of hours of paid work, in light of the expectation to be a 'good mother':

> 'We're doing a massive job anyway, and sanctioning us is only causing more stress upon us than there is already

> now in society. It's massive. And the expectations of being a good mum and, you know, if you're not doing what's right, then, no, sanctioning mums, no.' (Michelle, single mother, two children aged 9 and 7, wave one)

There is the implication in this comment that failing to meet the requirements of being a 'good mother' incurs stigma. Therefore, fulfilling the mandatory work-related requirements within Universal Credit can limit mothers' ability to fulfil caring responsibilities and therefore render them subject to societal condemnation. This is problematic given the stigma that single parents receiving benefits face (Jun, 2019). The evidence reinforces concerns that Universal Credit may exacerbate such stigma and also the tensions between unpaid care and paid work single mothers already encounter (Cain, 2016).

The work-related requirements of Universal Credit and paid work also negatively impacted the participants' mood and tiredness levels, and therefore their interactions with their children. As the work-related requirements were often incompatible with caring responsibilities, some of the mothers stayed up late in order to fulfil their requirements, resulting in tiredness. Also, many of the mothers reported feelings of stress arising from dual expectations of work-related requirements and caring responsibilities, and the possibility of sanctions for failure to meet requirements (see also Johnsen and Blenkinsopp, 2018). Although Kirsty felt her work coach was understanding of her caring responsibilities when her work-related requirements were set, she still experienced stress on account of having to fulfil her requirements:

> 'It's overwhelming, kind of especially when you feel like you've got to run a house, you've got to bring children up, then you've also got to make sure that you're putting everything in your journal and don't miss anything out. And then you're worried that I didn't do, I'm an hour

> missing, am I going to get sanctioned for that?' (Kirsty, single mother, two children aged 7 and 5, wave two)

The mothers explained how the impacts of the work-related requirements and paid work on their tiredness and mood in turn negatively affected their interactions with their children:

> 'I'm tired and then I'm snappy … you have to do that expectation otherwise you won't get that money, which then has a knock-on effect on your children because you can't give them what they need, but it also has an effect on your mood, your attitude, your well-being, everything, because you're worried, you're anxious. And I worry daily, so that will have a knock-on effect on your children.' (Michelle, single mother, two children aged 9 and 7, wave one)

> 'He [work coach] was like, "You know well you do need to be filling in your work thing, otherwise you're going to be sanctioned." So I felt like I had to fill in the work coach [sic] and show willing in every way I possibly could, which whenever I do work, it really affects my ability as a parent with [daughter] because I'm more shouty. I'm panicked and highly stressed all the time.' (Anna, single mother, one child aged 4, wave two)

The majority of the mothers who did not think that their caring responsibilities were negatively affected by the work-related requirements of Universal Credit either had an easement (and therefore were subject to reduced work-related requirements) or had a more equal share of the responsibility for childcare with their ex-partners. This finding that those with lesser work-related requirements or lesser responsibility for unpaid care did not consider their caring responsibilities to be negatively affected by the conditionality further demonstrates that a key issue for many mothers is the extensiveness of the work-related requirements within Universal Credit.

During the second wave of interviews, there was an increase in the number of mothers reporting negative impacts on caring responsibilities and also an increase in the range and extensiveness of the impacts mentioned. For the most part, this was because some mothers had moved into paid work and some had stopped their self-employed work and obtained positions as employees. At the second wave of interviews, Michelle had stopped her self-employed cleaning work on account of the difficulties of meeting the MIF (see Chapter Five) and had obtained a job as a carer in a residential home. Whereas previously she had been able to fit her paid work around her children, her new job entailed a shift pattern which affected her children, as she explained:

> 'So now I've got a job which is really quite difficult because the shift patterns are set at seven till half-two and twelve till eight, so that means now I'm having to rely on family and childminders and expect my children to get up at six o'clock in the morning too so that I can be at work. But that was the only job what offered more than 25 hours a week, so now I'm working 30 hours a week because I couldn't find a job that was 25 hours. ... With being self-employed, I had that flexibility. I had that flexibility where I could be there and then quickly there, cos I'd worked my whole diary around the children's schooling, their activities. Now I can't, I don't have that flexibility. I'm in one place and I'm not moving, so I can't do anything.' (Michelle, single mother, two children aged 10 and 7, wave two)

As the quote shows, Michelle was unable to obtain a job that was compatible with her caring responsibilities. Previous research has also shown that conditionality can push single mothers into applying for and accepting the first job that appears, regardless of compatibility with caring responsibilities (Graham and McQuaid, 2014). This indicates a problem with conditionality policies which focus on moving claimants quickly into any paid work rather than on helping them into work that is appropriate to their circumstances.

Some of those who had undertaken paid work since the start of their Universal Credit claim made some of the most pertinent comments about the impacts on their caring responsibilities:

> '[Youngest child is] like, "Mummy you don't play with us", and it breaks my heart but I have to come in, I have to cook tea. As soon as they come in, they've been at school, they'll have been two hours at after-school club, then they'll have had to walk home. They want to spend a bit of time with me. I can't because I have to then go off in the kitchen and stick the telly on to keep them, you know, quiet or … and yeah it does impact on the quality of time.' (Jessica, single mother, two children aged 6 and 5, wave two)

> 'When I've worked last week today she [daughter] was like, "Just spend the day with Mummy please", and it's really heart-breaking when you're like, "No you're off to nursery", and she's like, "No just Mummy's house today".' (Laura, single mother, one child aged 2, wave one)

Whereas self-employed work and mandatory job search activity afforded a degree of flexibility, obtaining paid work as an employee resulted in more rigid schedules and therefore had a greater impact on the mothers' caring responsibilities.

While the mothers who entered paid work did highlight various benefits of paid work (discussed further in Chapter Five), few spoke of ways paid work positively impacted their children. Two of the mothers stated that being in paid work benefited their children materially – for example, in terms of the presents the mothers were able to buy for them and the possibility of going on holiday – and a further two spoke of how being in paid work provided a positive role model for their children. Overall, the study's findings correspond with previous research which found that while there can be positive benefits of entering paid work for single-parent families, there can also be disadvantages in terms of loss of time spent with children, more complex schedules and increased tensions within the household (Millar and Ridge, 2009, 2020; Jun, 2015).

This analysis, which shows the negative impacts of work-related requirements and paid work on caring responsibilities, adds to criticisms of the assumption underlying current policy that paid work is universally in the best interests of claimants (Patrick, 2012). This assumption is also central to Universal Credit, which is designed to both promote and replicate the world of paid work (Millar and Bennett, 2017). More specifically, the extension of job search requirements to lead carers with a youngest child aged 3 or 4 was justified on the grounds that it would result in parents moving into paid work quicker, leading to increased well-being of children and their parents (DWP, 2015c). However, the findings show that these assertions are problematic as they do not acknowledge the ways paid work can be detrimental to both parents and their children (see also Crisp, Batty and Cole, 2009). The findings show that work-related requirements, such as job search activity, also have negative impacts on caring responsibilities, as under Universal Credit these are extensive and are accompanied by the pressure and stress of the possibility of being sanctioned (see also Johnsen and Blenkinsopp, 2018).

Challenges of taking children to the Jobcentre Plus

While several of the mothers were able to make sure they did not have to take their children to the JCP with them, this was unavoidable for many of the mothers. The overwhelming majority of mothers who took their children to the JCP with them for appointments found this difficult, with several referring to it as a "nightmare". Many of the mothers commented on the lack of facilities (such as toilets and children's books and toys) and the inappropriate atmosphere:

> 'They have no facilities. I remember [youngest child] getting a dirty nappy just before we needed to go in. I remember asking. They had no changing facilities: "No you can't use our toilets, the nearest place is Sainsbury's across the road."' (Jessica, single mother, two children aged 6 and 4, wave one)

> 'There's no toys for the children to play with. You have to give them your phone or bring a book or something like that, whereas it would be really relevant to have a nice child-friendly area. That would be really, really supportive, because otherwise it's a really austere place to be bringing a child.' (Anna, single mother, one child aged 4, wave one)

Many of the mothers commented that their children got bored and frustrated at the JCP, and they found keeping their children occupied and managing their behaviour while attending appointments challenging. These difficulties were exacerbated by the feeling of being watched by their work coach and other people in the JCP. 'Lisa', who had been in care herself and had recently experienced social services involvement in her family life on account of her ex-partner's behaviour towards their daughter, explained:

> 'I just gave her a banana to keep her quiet, keep her occupied, obviously cos it is boring sitting there listening to everything that they have to tell you … trying to keep a nearly-2-year-old busy, it's not easy … sometimes it's easier just to say yes to get it over with, just so you can

> get out of that situation, cos you don't want everybody looking at you and feeling tense that she's misbehaving cos she's bored.' (Lisa, single mother, one child aged 2, wave one)

Similarly, research conducted in New Zealand found that single mothers felt that their parenting was being surveyed during appointments at the Work and Income offices, which contributed to the oppressive atmosphere of the offices (Gray, 2017). The finding that there was an absence of an appropriate environment for children within the JCP further demonstrates the lack of recognition and consideration of caring responsibilities within the Universal Credit conditionality regime. The failure to accommodate children within the JCP put the mothers in challenging circumstances wherein, under the gaze of both staff and other claimants, they had to look after their children while participating in mandatory appointments. At times, this led to them making compromises in their parenting and incurred stress and embarrassment. Lisa cited the JCP environment as evidence of how the Universal Credit conditionality regime does not value mothers' caring roles. There were further reasons why the mothers felt their caring roles were devalued in the Universal Credit system, as discussed in the next section.

Mismatched views: the valuing of unpaid care

The adoption of policies that attempt to increase mothers' participation in the paid labour market may underestimate women's commitment to unpaid care and, through focusing on paid employment, fail to consider and value unpaid care (McDowell, 2005). The study's findings show how these claims are relevant to the conditionality within Universal Credit. This section outlines the participants' valuing of their unpaid caring roles and then details their views on the devaluing of care within the Universal Credit system.

Participants' valuing of unpaid care

The participants highly valued their unpaid caring roles (see also Duncan and Edwards, 1999; Lynch and Lyons, 2009). Many of the mothers prioritised the unpaid care of their children over paid work:

> 'Job's not everything … kids come first.' (Leanne, single mother, three children aged 12, 10 and 5, wave one)

> 'My children is like diamond for me, you see. I gonna look after my children first.' (Jamila, single mother, two children aged 7 and 5, wave one)

Several of the mothers referred to parenting as a "job", and many spoke of the hard work involved in caring for children. As the comments later demonstrate, the mothers considered their unpaid care to be an important contribution in the present and also for the future:

> 'I get great satisfaction out of everything, like knowing that I've done it all. It makes me proud. If I've achieved something, I know it's that I know my kids are well looked after.' (Michelle, single mother, two children aged 10 and 7, wave two)

> 'It's the best job in the world. It's the best thing you can do in your life, honest to God … it's a human being that's going to, hopefully if you've done the job correctly, they're going to do something good in the world.' (Leanne, single mother, three children aged 13, 10 and 5, wave two)

These comments show the pride some of the mothers took in this role. For some of the mothers, this was a role they wanted to fulfil themselves:

> 'I want to look after them, I don't want anybody else to look after them. That's why I chose to be a mum, to be a mum to them.' (Nicola, single mother, three children aged 18, 16 and 10, wave two)

While many of the mothers spoke of caring for their children as a "job" or in terms of "work", they also highlighted the relational and interdependent nature of caring (Bowlby et al, 2010; Williams, 2012), which distinguishes unpaid care from paid work, including paid care work (Cantillon and Lynch, 2017). For example, many of the mothers spoke about their desire to "be there" for their children (Ribbens McCarthy and Edwards, 2002). Also, some spoke of their love for their children and the time spent with them:

> 'Obviously he's a pain in the backside, as they all are, but you know he's my world and I won't be without him.' (Natasha, single mother, one child aged 14, wave one)

> 'I really enjoy doing stuff with the children and spending time with them.' (Lucy, single mother, two children aged 9 and 7, wave two)

These findings demonstrate that the mothers considered their caring roles to be an important part of their identities and roles they wanted to carry out (albeit with variations in the desired balance between paid work and unpaid care). For many of the mothers, these roles were a source of enjoyment, pride and satisfaction (Gillies, 2007; Holloway and Pimlott-Wilson, 2016). The mothers' caring roles were also seen as a significant responsibility entailing hard work and challenges (Lynch and Walsh, 2009), which questions portrayals of benefit recipients by the media and in the government literature as inactive and irresponsible (Patrick, 2017). The findings regarding the relational and affective aspects of unpaid care also point to the problematic assumption within the government discourse that care is a barrier to paid work and can be fully commodified (Lynch and Walsh, 2009).

Views on whether unpaid care is valued within the Universal Credit system

While the mothers highly valued their caring roles, 20 out of the 24 mothers said they did not think unpaid care was valued in the Universal Credit system. There were a variety of reasons given for this. Some of these reasons concerned the lack of discussion about their children in meetings with work coaches, the lack of personalisation of work-related requirements, the unrealistic expectations placed on them and the lack of choice regarding engagement in paid work (see Chapter Six). A particularly common response was the emphasis on paid work within the Universal Credit system:

> 'It just seems that they want everybody to be out working now, regardless of what you do or … your role as a parent, as a mother. They think you should be out working.' (Nicola, single mother, three children aged 18, 16 and 9, wave one)

There were indications that unpaid care did not just routinely fail to receive value in the Universal Credit system, but also incurred shame and exacerbated the stigma that single mothers in particular face:

> 'I think that it's sort of, you're looked down on, to be honest.' (Aisha, single mother, one child aged 10, wave one)

> 'You don't feel good when you're a single mum on Universal Credit. It's … almost, like I say, like frowned upon.' (Natasha, single mother, one child aged 14, wave two)

'Natasha', quoted earlier, highly valued her role as a mother but found this sense of pride in what she had achieved difficult to sustain when receiving a strong impression from the Universal Credit system that her unpaid caring role was not valued and was "almost something to be embarrassed of":

> 'You know, I try to be positive about it and think you're right, I am a mum and I've achieved all this and I have got these skills, and I could put them to good use. And then they just kind of pop your bubble and you think well, yeah, I am just a mum really, when you should be celebrating it. But, yeah, they don't really encourage, you know, you don't feel like you've achieved something. If you'd've gone on a course and done all these skills, then you know you get certificates and stuff, but because you've earnt them through being a mum, it's like, well, so what?' (Natasha, single mother, one child aged 14, wave two)

Overall, these findings correspond with prior research which found that mothers felt their unpaid caring roles were devalued within conditionality policies and objected to this (Patrick, 2014; Johnsen, 2016). These findings also suggest that social security policies play a part in constituting mothers' identities (Pulkingham et al, 2010). The current attempted shift to the adult worker model has been criticised for seeking to change mothers' gendered identities from carers to workers despite the importance some mothers attach to their caring identities (Holloway and Pimlott-Wilson, 2016). Similarly, Wright (2012) argues that welfare-to-work policies, through stigmatising those who are not in paid work, crowd out activities that are central to some mothers' identities. These criticisms were reflected in the findings that caring roles, which were important to the mothers' identities, were devalued – and, in some cases, stigmatised – within a system that almost exclusively prioritised paid work. This caused considerable discomfort for the mothers, as they were subject to a conditionality regime that was at odds with their values. While many of the mothers resented the devaluing of the unpaid care they provided, there were indications that a strong motherhood identity could be difficult to maintain in the face of the heavy emphasis on paid work and the compulsion within the Universal Credit conditionality regime.

Conclusion

This chapter has demonstrated that the conditionality for lead carers within Universal Credit significantly affects women's roles and responsibilities regarding unpaid care. The main effects on the mothers' caring responsibilities included limiting time to undertake caring responsibilities, increasing tensions in interactions with children and experiencing difficulties in taking children to the JCP, therefore reducing the quality of care the mothers were able to provide. The longitudinal analysis shows that the impacts were sustained over time and often exacerbated by entrance into paid work. Some of the women also experienced shame and stigma on account of undertaking unpaid care, and there were indications that women's caring identities may be eroded by the implementation of conditionality. For some mothers, having a work coach who had an understanding of caring responsibilities mediated some of the negative practical and emotional effects of the work-related requirements on mothers' caring responsibilities. However, on the whole, the work coaches had a limited impact on the most salient aspects of the work-related requirements and their subsequent impacts. The findings demonstrate that the negative impacts on caring responsibilities were derived from the almost exclusive emphasis within the Universal Credit conditionality regime on paid work alongside a failure to recognise and take into account caring responsibilities.

The findings show that there are broader implications of the conditionality within Universal Credit for women's citizenship roles and responsibilities in respect of unpaid care and paid work. While unpaid care has not historically been comprehensively valued in citizenship frameworks, there has been some recognition of caring responsibilities within the UK social security system: formerly, mothers could claim unconditional benefits on the basis of their unpaid caring responsibilities (Daly, 2011; Davies, 2015). The increasing application of conditionality over the past 20 years, which has culminated in the intensified and expanded conditionality under Universal Credit, removes this recognition and subsequently hinders, rather than promotes, the recognition of unpaid care as a valid societal contribution. By failing to recognise unpaid care, conditionality furthers the conception of paid work as the primary duty of the responsible citizen (Patrick, 2012), a notion that is highly gendered given women's disproportionate responsibility for unpaid care. The next chapter considers the implications of the conditionality within Universal Credit for mothers' employment trajectories and, subsequently, the extent to which conditionality helps them to obtain citizenship status through paid work.

FIVE

Universal Credit and paid work: "you can job search and job search and not get anywhere"

Introduction

While women have entered the paid labour force in significant numbers since the 1970s, they have mainly obtained part-time jobs and remain primarily responsible for unpaid care (Lewis, 2009; Boyer et al, 2017; Neitzert, 2020). Therefore, despite women's increasing participation in the paid labour market, they are still disadvantaged in social security systems and the dominant citizenship framework, as full-time paid work continues to be privileged (Lister, 2003). The predominant feminist approach to improving women's citizenship status has been to encourage women's full participation in the paid labour market (Jensen and Møberg, 2017). While there are disadvantages to this approach – for example, it may result in the continued failure to recognise the value and necessity of unpaid care – it does recognise the importance of paid work to women's economic security and independence.

Conditionality may initially appear to improve women's participation in the paid labour market; however, there are concerns that the application of conditionality to mothers exacerbates women's disadvantaged position in the paid labour market (Grover, 2007; MacLeavy, 2007; Grabham and Smith, 2010; Letablier et al, 2011; MacLeavy, 2011; Ingold and Etherington, 2013). A key concern is the lack of consideration within conditionality policies of existing gender inequalities in the paid labour market and the related gendered division of unpaid care, which can constrain and complicate women's participation in paid work (MacLeavy, 2011; Ingold and Etherington, 2013; Bennett and Daly, 2014; Davies, 2015). To investigate the conditionality within Universal Credit in light of these concerns, this chapter explores how the conditionality for lead carers within Universal Credit affects mothers' employment trajectories in respect of whether they obtain and sustain paid work and the types of paid work they obtain. The chapter starts by outlining the participants' paid work aspirations and barriers to paid work. The next two sections discuss, respectively, the formal childcare provision within Universal Credit and the employment-related support the participants received in obtaining paid work. The next section details the participants' experiences of trying to meet the work-related requirements of Universal Credit. The final section discusses the effects of the conditionality within Universal Credit on the participants' employment and earnings over time.

Paid work aspirations and barriers

A key assumption underlying the implementation of conditionality is that social security claimants prefer to receive their income in the form of social security benefits rather than earnings and, therefore, need to be motivated through the threat of sanction to undertake paid work (see Chapter Three). References to this perceived culture of 'worklessness' and 'welfare dependency' are found in the Universal Credit government literature (DWP, 2010a, 2010c, 2014a). Contrary to this narrative, over the course of the study, all of the mothers expressed the desire to enter paid work either in the present or near future:

> 'I'll work … I don't want to be stuck at home. I don't think any single parent does, because oh my God it makes you mental.' (Leanne, single mother, three children aged 13, 10 and 5, wave two)

While some of the mothers did not want to enter paid work immediately, on account of their caring responsibilities or studies, and there was variation in the amount of hours the mothers wanted to work, the overwhelming majority had specific paid work aspirations. Some of these mothers explained they did not want just any job and that they would like to train for a job that would result in higher earnings and a career. Kirsty, who had left school at the age of 14, explained:

> 'I don't just want to go back into a job that I don't enjoy. I want to get some training behind me, like better myself. Make sure that I'm going to do a good job before I actually do go into a job.' (Kirsty, single mother, two children aged 7 and 5, wave one)

Overall, the findings show that the assumption that claimants are unmotivated to undertake paid work and therefore need to be coerced into employment is flawed, as the mothers were motivated to enter paid work and had specific paid work aspirations (see also Wright and Patrick, 2019). The assumption that benefit claimants lack motivation to undertake paid work not only places the blame for unemployment on individuals but also diverts attention from structural and personal barriers to unemployment (Deacon and Patrick, 2011; Wright, 2012; Friedli and Stearn, 2015). In this study, the participants highlighted multiple barriers to paid work, as shown in Table 5.1.

Table 5.1: Participants' barriers to paid work

Participant	Childcare issues	Incompatibilities between available jobs and formal childcare provision	Lack of part-time jobs	Lack of jobs in the local area	Age	Lack of qualifications	Lack of work experience	Lack of skills	Lack of confidence	Lack of transport	Health conditions
Louise	■					■					
Lucy	■										
Jennifer	■										
Lisa	■	■									
Laura	■	■					■				
Angela	■	■									
Jodie										■	■
Helen	■					■			■	■	■
Ellie	■						■		■	■	■
Aisha	■	■	■	■					■	■	■
Claire		■									
Christina	■										

(continued)

Table 5.1: Participants' barriers to paid work (continued)

Participant	Childcare issues	Incompatibilities between available jobs and formal childcare provision	Lack of part-time jobs	Lack of jobs in the local area	Age	Lack of qualifications	Lack of work experience	Lack of skills	Lack of confidence	Lack of transport	Health conditions
Jamila	■	■				■		■			
Emily	■	■		■							
Nicola		■									
Anna	■	■		■	■	■	■	■	■	■	■
Jessica	■	■	■	■	■	■	■	■	■	■	■
Zoe	■										
Michelle	■	■									
Kelly	■										
Natasha	■		■	■	■		■				
Kirsty	■		■	■					■	■	■
Danielle	■	■									
Leanne	■	■	■			■			■	■	■

As the table shows, a key barrier to paid work faced by the overwhelming majority of the mothers concerned childcare. Lisa described the difficulties she faced in accessing childcare:

> 'This nursery has no foot space on the days that she's not there, and even if they did, it's … three hundred quid a month just on that nursery fee, so I don't have that spare.' (Lisa, single mother, one child aged 2, wave one)

Others also mentioned the prohibitive cost of childcare, even with the extra government provision (discussed later). For many of the other mothers, there was also a lack of available childcare. This was particularly acute during school holidays.

An issue raised by many of the mothers was the incompatibility between available jobs, which often required flexible working or nonstandard hours, and the hours of formal childcare provision. Many mothers spoke of the impracticalities of carrying out jobs that require early morning, evening and weekend work given the unavailability of formal childcare provision at these times. Lisa went on to explain the infeasibility of reentering the job she undertook before having her daughter:

> 'Before I had [child], I used to work like half past seven in the morning till like one or three or five. So I'm not going to get childcare for half past seven in the morning unless I do, like, the evening shifts, but even some of them are like three till ten, so there again it doesn't quite fit in. Obviously I can't really do nights cos they're like seven till seven, and who's going to watch her at seven on a night?' (Lisa, single mother, one child aged 2, wave one)

This finding points to the difficulties mothers face when trying to enter a gendered paid labour market that operates on the assumption that workers are unrestricted by caring responsibilities (Conaghan, 2009). It also shows that the changing paid labour market, which involves demand for flexible workers and an increase in jobs of nonstandard hours, has exacerbated these difficulties (Cain, 2016). Additionally, it demonstrates that formal childcare provision can only facilitate entrance into paid work to a limited extent given the mismatch between the hours of formal childcare provision and the hours of paid work (Javornik and Ingold, 2015).

In line with previous research (Haux, 2012), many of the other mothers also faced multiple barriers to paid work. The research findings suggest that for some participants, the combination of multiple barriers made entering paid work almost impossible. Natasha, who had a long-term health condition, explained:

> 'I'm limited as to what I can do job wise, and you go on Indeed and, you know, three thousand jobs, but then you refine it, so it's like ten hours and then within a ten-mile radius and then there's only admin and reception kind of work. But the majority of them you need to have previous experience in it, and even though I've worked in customer service all my life, I've never been a receptionist.' (Natasha, lone mother, one child aged 14, wave two)

As Natasha's comment highlights, for some mothers, the paid work expectations of Universal Credit may be unrealistic given the availability of jobs, particularly part-time jobs. Research conducted by the single-parent charity Gingerbread (Dewar and Ben-Galim, 2017) investigating the conditionality within Universal Credit for parents of 3- and 4-year-olds similarly found that there is a lack of part-time jobs. Therefore the charity has argued that conditionality requirements should be suspended until appropriate jobs (and also sufficient formal childcare) are in place.

Overall, the findings indicate that the unemployed status or low earnings of the mothers were due to the multiple and significant barriers to paid work they faced, rather than

individual problems with motivation or behaviour (see also Patrick, 2011; Graham and McQuaid, 2014; Johnsen, 2016). Childcare was a particularly pertinent barrier faced by the mothers, regardless of cultural capital and relationship status. The next section explores the extent to which the increased formal childcare provision within Universal Credit helped the mothers obtain paid work.

Universal Credit childcare provision

Under Universal Credit, there has been an increase in state assistance with formal childcare provision. Universal Credit claimants can claim back up to 85 per cent of their childcare costs (DWP, 2020e), which is an increase from the 70 per cent provided under Working Tax Credit. However, the mothers who tried to access this provision invariably encountered difficulties (see also Griffiths et al, 2020). A key problem was lack of communication about the help with childcare costs within Universal Credit (see also DWP, 2017b; Wood, 2021):

> 'So I don't know where I'm going to stand of how much they'll cover for me with our income. There's nobody that's discussed it with you. There's nobody that tells you if you get a job and you're on £8.50 an hour and you pay this much on childcare, we'll give you this so much for your childcare and you'll be on this much from work.' (Kelly, coupled mother, two children aged 4 and 2, wave one)

Another common problem, as documented by charities (for example, McDonough, 2019; McKechnie, 2019), was the requirement to pay formal childcare costs upfront. Under Universal Credit, parents are required to pay childcare costs themselves and report them retrospectively to the DWP each month (DWP, 2020c). They are then reimbursed in a subsequent Universal Credit payment. 'Anna' explained how this made entering paid work difficult:

> 'You've got to [get to] that level where you've saved to pay them in advance, so you can't even get a job until you've saved some money, and you can't save any money because there's no spare money.' (Anna, single mother, one child aged 4, wave one)

Some of the mothers said they were put off trying to find paid work or more paid work in part because of the requirement to pay childcare fees upfront. Others reported that paying the fees upfront resulted in financial hardship or debt. The reimbursement of childcare costs was not just a problem at the start of the Universal Credit claim. For example, 'Jennifer' entered paid work several months after making a claim for Universal Credit but found that she could not continue in her job due to the fact she was paid her childcare costs in arrears:

> 'It wasn't really a sustainable thing for me to be doing, because it cost more per hour for the childminder than I made per hour from the [company]. And even though I could claim back some of that money, it was after I'd already paid for it, so I was just always out of pocket … so I ended up quitting the job because it just wasn't sustainable paying for the childcare.' (Jennifer, single mother, two children aged 6 and 3, wave one)

Overall, these findings show that increased assistance with childcare costs did not help many of the mothers overcome the barrier childcare posed to entering paid work, and for a couple of mothers, the delivery of this provision made paid work impossible to sustain (see also Work and Pensions Committee, 2018b; McDonough, 2019; Griffiths et al, 2020). They also support the contention that childcare cannot be fully commodified, from a practical as well as a relational standpoint

(Fraser, 1998; Lewis and Giullari, 2005). This is problematic given that governments have turned to formal childcare provision in order to remove female 'barriers' to employment (Lewis and Giullari, 2005). More broadly, this supports the claim that some women will always be disadvantaged in the paid labour market as all of women's responsibility for unpaid care cannot be transferred to formal childcare provision (Fraser, 1998).

Employment-related support

The government has claimed that under Universal Credit, claimants receive tailored support, principally delivered through work coaches (DWP, 2014a). The government aims to provide claimants with the same work coach throughout their Universal Credit claim so that a relationship can be built between the claimant and the work coach (DWP, 2014a). According to government literature, work coaches have been trained to listen to claimants and help them think through their paid work aspirations and overcome barriers to paid work (DWP, 2014a). This section explores the limited extent to which these claims were realised in the mothers' experiences of employment support.

Work coach relationships and support

For the most part, the mothers were positive about their work coaches. Of the 24 mothers, 15 had a positive relationship with their work coaches, 2 had a mixed relationship and 5 had a negative relationship, while 2 had minimal contact with their work coaches. Those who had an easement tended to have particularly positive relationships with their work coaches. 'Helen', who had an easement on account of ongoing health problems following experiences of domestic abuse, explained:

> 'She's lovely. She'll just say, "You know you're with me and you don't have to worry".' (Helen, single mother, two children aged 13 and 11)

However, there were variations in whether the participants had the same work coach throughout their claim. While some of the participants had the same work coach, others saw different people throughout their claim:

> 'Being passed from pillar to post. Nobody knows your circumstances so you have to explain it every time you go.' (Kelly, coupled mother, two children aged 4 and 2, wave one)

Previous research has highlighted the importance to single mothers of the character and consistency of the relationship between JCP advisers and claimants (Haux et al, 2012; Graham and McQuaid, 2014). Therefore, while the prevalence in the current study of participants who had a good relationship with their work coach is positive, concerns remain for those who had negative relationships and those who had a number of different work coaches.

Despite the majority of the participants stating they had a good relationship with their work coaches, most also reported that they did not receive any support, advice or training from their work coaches or the JCP in relation to finding paid work; this is in contrast to the government literature (DWP, 2014a). Over the two waves of interviews, many of the mothers explained that their meetings with their work coaches were mainly concerned with checking that they had fulfilled their mandatory requirements, rather than with providing employment-related support:

> 'They ask you what you're doing. They don't give you any help bar asking what you're doing, and they're ticking a box.' (Leanne, single mother, three children aged 13, 10 and 5, wave two)

On occasions, support was not provided even when participants asked for it:

> 'An' I did ring up about the lollipop lady [job] cos I thought I could do that, and I rang I think the Jobcentre up, and they said, "Oh you need to ring the council for that," and put the phone down. I was like, oh right, that was a quick call, okay. Yeah so I didn't bother applying for it in the end.' (Angela, single mother, two children aged 8 and 5, wave one)

A minority of the mothers received a limited amount of support and training – for example, help with writing or updating their CVs – or had been told about training courses and support provided by external agencies. While some of the mothers found the assistance with CV writing helpful and three were signposted to external agencies and courses that were beneficial, a larger proportion of the sample thought that the support offered was too basic or unhelpful. Only one mother reported that she had received substantial support and training in obtaining paid work. This mother's work coach pointed her towards job vacancies that were compatible with her work experience and caring responsibilities, and she also attended a helpful course provided by the JCP.

These findings, which show little meaningful support was given to the claimants and that there was an emphasis on surveillance rather than support, correspond with much prior research on conditionality in the UK (Haux et al, 2012; Whitworth, 2012; Patrick, 2017; Dwyer, 2018a). Therefore, while the government has stated that under Universal Credit there is an increase in support to find paid work, provided in return for increased paid work expectations under Universal Credit (DWP, 2014a), this study shows that the work-related requirements have increased but the levels of employment-related support have not. The analysis suggests that the onus is on the claimant to find paid work, under the threat of sanction for noncompliance. Thus, as well as individualising the 'problem' of unemployment, the government is individualising the 'solution', regardless of the barriers claimants face in obtaining paid work.

Support for long-term paid work aspirations

As previously discussed, the overwhelming majority of the mothers had specific paid work aspirations. However, contrary to the government literature (DWP, 2014a), for the most part, work coaches did not ask the participants about their paid work aspirations. In response to a question regarding whether her work coach had asked about her paid work aspirations, Zoe answered:

> 'No, no, no, no, that's silly. That would be a sensible question to ask! Because if they asked that question to everybody, then they could actually work out an actual plan of how to get that person to that point instead of forcing them out every week to apply for jobs that they don't want and that they'll have absolutely no intention of working their best at if it's a rubbish job.' (Zoe, single mother, two children aged 14 and 7, wave two)

Some participants reported that they had informed their work coaches of their paid work aspirations. However, there was little evidence that the work coaches supported the mothers in achieving these aspirations, and at times the work coaches appear to have disregarded them. For example, 'Jamila' aspired to be a chef; however, despite having told her work coach of this aim, she was not given any support in working towards it and instead was mandated to apply for a job in a newsagent. Similarly, when other participants were either directed towards or encouraged to enter particular jobs, they tended to be gendered, low-status, low-paid, insecure jobs in areas such as paid care work, childminding, hairdressing, fast food and retail (see also Smith et al, 2008; Grant, 2009; Ingold and Etherington, 2013).

Some of the mothers explicitly expressed the view that Universal Credit does not support the achievement of long-term career aspirations:

> 'I think it's not supported me in terms of thinking what the best thing to do career-wise is. It's made me, and it's probably the same for a lot of people, think gosh, quick, what can I do, because immediately you have these requirements and you're thinking ooh what is it that I can do to earn money. So you're maybe not thinking about the best thing to do or the most long-term plan. It's a very now, now [bangs table] thing, and in a sense the idea is that any paid work is better than no paid work, whether that's relevant for your skills or for long term or fitting round the kids. So I don't think it's supportive of longer-term aspirations.' (Lucy, single mother, two children aged 9 and 7, wave two)

Previous research has also found that the demands of conditionality can hinder realisation of long-term paid work aspirations (Patrick, 2017). This study contributes to concerns about the work first approach and also shows the gendered issues of this approach. As women occupy a disadvantaged position in the paid labour market and mothers in particular are more likely to undertake low-paid work (Reis, 2018), they especially need to be supported in obtaining long-term, sustainable, adequately paid work. However, the work first approach emphasises getting claimants into paid work at the first opportunity and, therefore, may further women's disadvantaged position in the paid labour market through failing to support them to achieve their long-term paid work aspirations.

Experiences of meeting work-related requirements

The lack of employment-related support is particularly problematic given that the overwhelming majority of the mothers faced difficulties in meeting the work-related requirements attached to their Universal Credit claim. The mothers encountered a variety of challenges. A common issue was the difficulty of carrying out work-related requirements as well as caring responsibilities:

> 'He's [her son] engaging in conversation with me and I'm breaking off, and again, you know, it doesn't work. It just doesn't work really. You can't focus on what you're doing, you've got one eye on your children or you're getting interrupted every two minutes: "Can I have a drink? Can I have this?" And you just think, oh, I give up.' (Jessica, single mother, two children aged 6 and 4, wave one)

This finding demonstrates that the lack of recognition of caring responsibilities when the Claimant Commitment was formed and during ongoing interactions with work coaches (see Chapter Four) negatively impacted not only the mothers' caring responsibilities but also their ability to carry out work-related requirements. This reflects criticisms that conditionality policies fail to account for the gendered division of labour and do not recognise how this can create difficulties for mothers in engaging in the paid labour market (MacLeavy, 2011; Ingold and Etherington, 2013; Bennett and Daly, 2014; Davies, 2015).

For the most part, the coupled mothers had additional responsibility for fulfilling work-related requirements. All but one of the seven mothers with experience of a joint claim helped their partners with their work-related commitments – for example, by looking for jobs and reporting job search activity, or ensuring they fulfilled certain mandatory tasks:

> 'He was a little bit useless. I filled in his job search for him.' (Danielle, single mother, two children, aged 7 and 6, wave one)

> 'I can see on the page if we need to go, like go to the Jobcentre, if we need to do something. So I'll get a text and it'll tell me something's up there, an' then I'll check

> it, an' if he needs to do something, I'll be like, "Do it, do it right now, do it straight away, don't leave it, do it."' (Jodie, coupled mother, one child aged 5, wave one)

The coupled mothers helped their partners with their work-related requirements to avoid a sanction, because the whole family is likely to be impacted if one member of the couple receives a sanction, due to the single payment into one account (Millar and Bennett, 2017). 'Emily', who did not help her partner with his mandatory requirements at the start of the change from a single claim to a joint claim, ended up having her Universal Credit claim closed:

> 'Where it fell down was the boyfriend didn't go to a key appointment that he was supposed to have gone to, and the next I heard about that was just a message on my phone. You just get a message saying: "Your Universal Credit claim has closed." … So I felt really pissed off because at that point I very much still felt like, well, it's my money, it's my claim. Yes we've moved in together, but this is still for me and my son, and he messed it up.' (Emily, single mother, one child aged 8, wave two)

This demonstrates one highly problematic aspect of the joint claim, wherein one partner can lose access to social security provision due to the behaviour of the other. While research commissioned by the DWP has reported that Universal Credit 'has been encouraging more collaborative job searching' among some couples (DWP, 2017b, p 61), this study, in line with previous research (Andersen, 2019), shows that such collaboration can be highly gendered, as the women helped the men with their work-related requirements. Research conducted by Griffiths et al (2020) has similarly found that female partners tend to take on more responsibility for managing the Universal Credit online claim. The additional responsibility women undertake for fulfilling work-related requirements and managing the online claim furthers the gendered imbalance in unpaid labour that coupled mothers experience.

Some mothers found the extent of the job search itself unrealistic due to the number of hours required and the lack of available suitable jobs (see also Wright and Patrick, 2019; Wright et al, 2020):

> 'Thirty hours actually is quite impossible where there's only so many websites that are available, there are only so many jobs that fit the criteria.' (Jessica, single mother, two children aged 6 and 5, wave two)

In addition to finding the job search itself challenging, some mothers also struggled to report their job search in their online journal or to fulfil administrative tasks. This was due to factors such as learning disabilities or lack of access to the internet or a computer:

> 'If you don't know computer[s], you know, online and stuff like that, it's really difficult. I find it difficult cos I'm dyslexic so, you know, that's even worse.' (Angela, single mother, two children aged 8 and 5, wave one)

> 'I find it quite hard to keep a track on how many jobs I've applied for … I've been finding it especially [hard] on my phone to then type it up onto, cos you have to put each job that you've been applying for.' (Aisha, single mother, one child aged 10, wave one)

These difficulties in meeting administrative tasks are very problematic under Universal Credit given that claimants face sanctions for failing to report their job search on their Universal Credit online journal and can face reductions or complete withdrawal of payments for failing to carry out other online tasks, such as reporting a variety of changes straight away (HMG, 2020). Additionally, those in paid employment still face the possibility of being sanctioned (even if they are not subject to requirements to increase their earnings) due to the administration required in maintaining Universal Credit claims. While the government has explained the online system is intended to increase claimants' responsibility for their claims and help them learn digital skills that will help them both search for and acquire jobs (DWP, 2012a, 2015b), this study suggests the online administration can significantly add to the hard work involved in claiming benefits (see also Patrick, 2017; Griffiths et al, 2020).

During the second wave of interviews, the mothers who were still subject to job search requirements reported that difficulties with meeting these requirements were ongoing and, in some cases, had increased due to the prolonged length of time they had spent job searching. For example, Natasha continued to experience difficulties given the lack of available jobs and the amount of time she was required to job search each week. Over time, meeting job search requirements became more difficult as she could not repeatedly apply for the same jobs:

> (Wave One) 'It's pretty difficult … there's only the reception work, admin and cashier. That narrows it down … you can't realistically, you can't spend ten hours looking for three specific type of jobs.'
>
> (Wave Two) 'Obviously I'm restricted as to what jobs I can look for, and they're very limited, part-time hours for the kind of jobs that I'm applying for. And they're few and far between. So I'm struggling to meet the ten-hour deadline … you're left with about 20 jobs that you can apply for, and then you've got to do another ten hours search the next week, and it's still the same 20 jobs and they don't change. So, you know, what am I supposed to do? I can't apply for the same job every single week cos I think the employer would get a bit peeved off.' (Natasha, single mother, one child aged 14)

For many of the self-employed mothers, the challenges of meeting work-related expectations had increased at the second wave of interviews, as they were no longer in their start-up year and were now subject to the MIF (see Chapter Three). Regardless of educational levels and professions, none of the self-employed mothers were consistently meeting this threshold. Various reasons were given for this, including difficulties in carrying out self-employed work during school holidays, the inadequacy of the one-year start-up period to establish and grow their businesses, and fluctuations in pay. Additionally, many of the mothers found they had to work many hours in order to meet the MIF due to the low pay they received and the type of work they were doing. Jennifer, who had not been able to sustain her job on account of the ongoing issues with claiming childcare costs in arrears, commented:

> 'I think that back when I first was planning to be a childminder and thought like, oh, no problem, I can work two days a week with two kids a day, that will fit right into everything else we're already doing. I think I was quite optimistic about that, and then of course the reality is of being a childminder is that, you know, kids all come on different days and parents are always changing what, you know, what they need. … I do have to work basically twice as much as my requirement.' (Jennifer, single mother, two children aged 6 and 3, wave two)

As Caraher and Reuter (2019) argue, in light of the increased likelihood of the self-employed having fluctuating earnings and the newly self-employed having lower earnings, the MIF along with the inadequacy of the start-up period is likely to exacerbate the material precarity of the self-employed. This study indicates there is a gendered dimension to these issues. The MIF is applied continuously, and there are no exemptions for periods of the year, such as the school holidays, when mothers are less able to undertake self-employed work. It

does not recognise the low pay of much typically gendered self-employed work (such as paid care work and cleaning). In addition, while mothers with a child under the age of 13 are subject to expectations of part-time paid work on account of their caring responsibilities, they are not given an extended start-up period to compensate for the fact they may have less hours available in the first year to establish and grow their businesses.

Overall, the analysis shows that many of the participants faced multiple challenges in meeting their work-related requirements in part due to the insufficient recognition of caring responsibilities within the Universal Credit conditionality regime. The longitudinal analysis shows that over time, difficulties in meeting work-related requirements continued and in some cases increased. As the mothers found meeting the work-related requirements difficult – and at times impossible – to fulfil, the conditionality may be of limited efficacy in moving the mothers into paid work or helping them increase their earnings. The next section details the changes in, or absences of, employment and earnings over the course of the study.

Effects of conditionality on employment and earnings

The government has stated in relation to gender that the conditionality within Universal Credit 'presents an opportunity to promote equality in work and narrow the employment gap' (DWP, 2012c, p 42). However, charities have highlighted the problematic combination of women's predominance in low-paid, insecure work and the emphasis in Universal Credit on moving people into any type of work at the first opportunity (Fawcett Society, 2015; Gingerbread, 2015). In this study, the requirement to take 'any work' was stipulated on the participants' Claimant Commitments and reiterated by several of their work coaches. This section explores the mothers' employment trajectories.

At the first wave of interviews, 3 of the 24 participants had moved into, and remained in, paid jobs since the start of their Universal Credit claim, a further 2 had entered self-employment and 1 had had a series of temporary jobs. Six of the other participants were already employed or self-employed at the start of their Universal Credit claim. Table 5.2 shows the participants' work status at the first and second waves of interviews.

As the table demonstrates, there was little change between the first and second waves of interviews. All of the participants were still in receipt of Universal Credit. A further two participants had obtained and maintained jobs. One of these mothers got a job as a paid carer for people with learning disabilities. Kirsty, who had been hoping to undertake more training to improve her career and earning prospects, obtained a cleaning job:

> 'It's like a zero hour contract what I'm on … it's cleaning at [event venue] so once the gig's finished at three o'clock in the morning, we can go straight in and clean, rather than waiting, and then we can get done by eleven.' (Kirsty, single mother, two children aged 7 and 5, wave two)

As well as Michelle (see Chapter Four), 'Louise' had moved from being self-employed to being employed. For those already in paid work, earnings had stayed the same, gone down or increased (for the most part, the increases were slight and none of them were sufficient for a move off Universal Credit):

> 'I think they [earnings] have sort of plateaued at the minute.' (Claire, single mother, two children aged 7 and 4, wave two)

> 'I got a new job which was being [council role] and that happened in May. The [charity] job ended in July time, so that was quite a nice swap over from one three-day[s]-a-week job, basically switch that for a different

Table 5.2: Changes in employment between the two waves of interviews

Participant	Wave 1	Wave 2
Louise	Self-employed carer/ cleaner, complementary therapist, product salesperson	Employed 24 hours a week in administration at a school, a limited amount of complementary therapies and product sales
Lucy	Self-employed writer/copy writer	Self-employed writer/ copy writer Increase in earnings some months but not meeting the MIF on a consistent basis
Jennifer	Self-employed childminder	Self-employed childminder Increase in earnings but not meeting the MIF on a consistent basis
Lisa	Unemployed	N/A
Laura	Recently undertook temporary work doing head counts, about to undertake temporary work in the Christmas period	Employed 21 hours a week in sales (temporary)
Angela	Employed 20 hours a week as a cleaner	Employed 20 hours a week as a cleaner Slight increase in hourly pay
Jodie	Unemployed	N/A
Helen	Unemployed	Unemployed
Ellie	Unemployed	Employed 16 hours a week as a carer
Aisha	Unemployed	N/A
Claire	Self-employed complementary therapist	Self-employed complementary therapist Earnings stayed the same, not meeting the MIF consistently

(continued)

Table 5.2: Changes in employment between the two waves of interviews (continued)

Participant	Wave 1	Wave 2
Christina	Self-employed doula, trainer, carer	Self-employed doula, trainer Decrease in earnings, not meeting the MIF consistently
Jamila	Unemployed	Unemployed
Emily	Zero-hours contract in academic support, self-employed office administrator and research assistant	Employed in a council role, self-employed in office administration and catering Hours stayed the same, decrease in earnings
Nicola	Self-employed hairdresser	Self-employed hairdresser Earnings stayed the same, not meeting the MIF consistently
Anna	Unemployed	Unemployed
Jessica	Employed 17 hours a week in administration	Employed 30 hours a week in administration Slight increase in hourly pay
Zoe	Full-time student (no summer paid work)	Full-time student (no summer paid work but also no work-related requirements)
Michelle	Self-employed cleaner	About to start a job as a carer (30 hours a week)
Kelly	Unemployed	N/A
Natasha	Unemployed	Unemployed
Kirsty	Unemployed	Employed as a cleaner, zero-hours contract (20–44 hours a week)
Danielle	Unemployed	Unemployed
Leanne	Employed 16 hours a week as a shop assistant	Employed one day a week as a shop assistant Zero-hours contract cleaning job (paid slightly higher) Working 16 hours a week in total

> three-day[s]-a-week job but for kind of half the money.' (Emily, single mother, one child aged 8, wave two)

> 'I've managed to increase my hours … it's an increase in pay as well … but as I said, I still, because I'm a single parent and I'm not earning a fortune, I still have a contribution from Universal Credit.' (Jessica, single mother, two children aged 6 and 5, wave two)

Five participants (of those reinterviewed and excluding the full-time student) were still unemployed at the second wave of interviews. Helen and Jamila described the difficulties of trying to obtain paid work:

> 'I put down only a couple of weeks ago about applying for that other job. And then cos that was within school hours, it was fantastic so … but I didn't hear a thing … so I thought, oh well, there'll be loads of people wanting school hours anyway … so I know I'm going to be having problems there.' (Helen, single mother, two children aged 13 and 11, wave two)

> 'I went to job fair, I took some papers, I ask them about for job the time I wanted, but they say no. Is impossible because they need me any time.' (Jamila, single mother, two children aged 8 and 5, wave two)

Of concern, all of the five participants who were still unemployed at the second wave of interviews had a health condition or had experienced domestic abuse, or both. In addition, four of these mothers had no family support and no contact with the children's fathers. Most lacked recent work experience. This suggests that conditionality is of particularly limited efficacy in moving those furthest from the paid labour market, and who have the most responsibility for unpaid care, into paid work. Another issue highlighted by the study was the difficulties in sustaining paid work. Over the course of the study, five mothers obtained jobs but did not keep them due to problems with the formal childcare provision within Universal Credit and health conditions.

The eight mothers who had entered paid work (employment, self-employment, or a series of temporary jobs) since the start of their Universal Credit claim and remained in work at the second wave of interviews were typically engaged in gendered, low-paid and insecure paid work, such as cleaning, caring, hairdressing, childminding and administration. One of the participants, who had a master's degree, obtained two roles since claiming Universal Credit that were of a higher status and less gendered. However, these roles were low-paid, and she undertook less secure, more gendered work alongside them. This participant was very overqualified for these other roles. Similarly, three of the other seven participants were overqualified for the jobs they obtained. Previous research has also found that single parents subject to conditionality tend to obtain low-paid, unsustainable jobs with limited prospects for career progression (Johnsen, 2016).

All of the mothers who entered paid work highlighted positives of their work. Some got a sense of achievement from working or found their particular job rewarding. Other positives included increased confidence, social interaction and the opportunity to be a role model for children. The main negatives cited were the detrimental impacts on their caring responsibilities and the tiredness and stress incurred (see Chapter Four). While some of the participants explained that they were able to provide for their children more materially as a result of paid work, others expressed resentment about the low pay they received. 'Ellie', who had entered paid care work, reported that while she found her work personally rewarding, as she was making a considerable difference to the people she cared for, she was not paid well enough for what she was doing. As this reflection indicates, the types of paid work the participants obtained are not intrinsically of low value, but are not valued in society due to the gendered cultural devaluation of the types of paid work women are concentrated in (Fraser, 1998). This study reinforces concerns that without a reevaluation of different types of paid work, compelling women into work through conditional benefits reproduces gendered economic inequalities (Grover, 2007).

The participants who moved into paid work mainly attributed this to their own motivation and efforts rather than to the conditionality within Universal Credit. Regarding the efficacy of conditionality and whether the work-related requirements had contributed to her move into paid work, 'Jessica' explained:

> 'It's a waste of everybody's time, I personally think … I had every intention of finding work, you know, which it would have been nicer to do in my own time really, rather than having … these demands put on me.' (Jessica, lone parent, two children aged 6 and 4, wave one)

Also, some participants thought that the conditionality negatively impacted their long-term career prospects through the emphasis on getting claimants into paid work quickly. Many participants considered that the job search requirements were futile, counterproductive or added unnecessary pressure (see also Dwyer, 2018a). Over time, there was a higher prevalence of mothers who stated they thought the conditionality within Universal Credit was counterproductive. These mothers had more prolonged experience of trying to meet work-related requirements by the second wave of interviews, and as the following quote indicates, this longer duration of being subject to conditionality resulted in increased detrimental impacts on attempts to obtain paid work:

> 'I don't think it's that helpful cos you can job search and job search and not get anywhere, and it can be even more discouraging.' (Danielle, single mother, two children aged 8 and 7, wave two)

The longitudinal analysis indicates that the conditionality within Universal Credit was largely ineffective in helping mothers enter secure, sustainable, adequately paid jobs and progress in paid work. This finding is consistent with prior research which found very limited evidence that conditionality improves sustained moves into employment and stimulates progression in the paid labour market (Goodwin, 2008; Reeves, 2017; Dwyer, 2018b). Regardless of education level, the vast majority of participants who obtained paid work entered gendered, low-paid, insecure, part-time work. This suggests that the conditionality within Universal Credit does not support women in obtaining jobs that improve their disadvantaged position in the paid labour market and can exacerbate this through the work first approach. Consequently, these findings reflect concerns that conditionality can entrench gender inequalities in the paid labour market (Grover, 2007; MacLeavy, 2007; Grabham and Smith, 2010; Letablier et al, 2011; MacLeavy, 2011).

Conclusion

This chapter has shown that the conditionality within Universal Credit had limited positive impact on the employment trajectories of these mothers. Key factors contributing to the lack of sustained moves into secure, adequately paid work and increases in earnings were the difficulties in accessing the formal childcare provision within Universal Credit and the absence of support received from work coaches and the JCP. While many of the participants had positive relationships with their work coaches, on the whole this did not result in increased moves into paid work as it was not accompanied by meaningful support. Of significance, the mothers who either currently or previously had an easement (due to experiences of domestic abuse or health conditions) were less likely to obtain paid work, in part because they were not ready to enter paid work or were not given the support they needed to overcome the substantial barriers they faced. The study also indicates that the lack of movements into adequately paid, secure, sustainable work is due to the work first approach. For some of the mothers, this limited opportunities for long-term career planning, and resulted in some taking the first job available regardless of compatibility with education, experience and caring responsibilities. Therefore, this study indicates that conditionality does not help improve women's disadvantaged position in the paid labour market and in some ways entrenches it further.

As the conditionality within Universal Credit is of limited efficacy in improving sustained moves into adequately paid work and can further women's disadvantaged labour market position, this policy has wider implications for women's access to social security rights and their citizenship status. As the Universal Credit conditionality regime did not help some of the mothers, particularly those furthest from the paid labour market, to secure paid work, this policy did not enable them to obtain employment-related social security rights or citizenship status. For the mothers subject to the conditionality within Universal Credit who did obtain paid work, the types of jobs they obtained did not confer sufficient pay, social standing or employment-related social security rights, and more broadly did not enable these mothers to obtain full citizenship status. Thus while the conditionality within Universal Credit furthers the gendered notion that citizenship status is only obtained through engagement in paid work, this policy is largely ineffective in enabling them to obtain citizenship status in its current gendered form. The next chapter discusses the implications of the conditionality within Universal Credit for women's agency.

SIX

Universal Credit and agency: "there's no element of choice"

Introduction

Agency refers to the ability to determine one's own daily life (Annesley, 2007) and relates to the capacity for free choice (Gould, 1983; Lister, 2003; Wright, 2012; McNay, 2016) (see Chapter Two). Enlarging women's ability to exercise agency regarding engagement in both unpaid care and paid work is a key aspect of creating a more gender-inclusive citizenship framework, given the importance of enabling women to participate in both unpaid care and paid work (see Chapter Two). Therefore, policies are needed that not only promote the valuing of unpaid care and women's position in the paid labour market but also enable women (and men) to make genuine choices regarding engagement in unpaid care and paid work (Lewis and Giullari, 2005). However, there have been concerns that rather than promoting genuine choice regarding unpaid care and paid work, conditionality may deny mothers the choice to carry out unpaid care and restrict their agency in regard to decisions about their engagement in the paid labour market (Grabham and Smith, 2010; Davies, 2012, 2015; Whitworth and Griggs, 2013; Rafferty and Wiggan, 2017; Millar, 2019). To investigate these concerns and how mothers respond to the compulsion within the Universal Credit regime, this chapter explores the extent to which mothers experience compulsion through being subject to the welfare conditionality within Universal Credit and how they respond to it over time.

This chapter starts by detailing the participants' work–care choices. It then investigates the extent to which the participants' Claimant Commitments were negotiated before discussing the participants' experiences of compulsion over time. Following this, the chapter explores the participants' views on the compulsion within Universal Credit and then discusses their responses to it. The final section explores the overall impacts of the compulsion on the participants' agency regarding engagement in unpaid care and paid work.

Participants' work–care choices

In line with previous research (for example, Thomas and Griffiths, 2006; Coleman and Riley, 2012), the majority of the participants reported that they wanted to undertake part-time paid work. While there was variation in the number of hours the mothers wanted to work, they consistently referred to wanting paid work that fitted in with their caring responsibilities:

> 'Children aren't a nine to five so, again, you have to work around them, not them work around you.' (Natasha, single mother, one child aged 14, wave one)

Prior research has also shown that single mothers want and need paid employment that fits around their caring responsibilities, described as 'work-fits-family and not family-fits-work' (Millar, 2019, p 91).

The longitudinal analysis shows that over time, there was very little change in the participants' work–care choices. During the second wave of interviews, the vast majority of participants stated their work–care choices had stayed the same.

For example, in both waves of interviews, Louise explained her preference for work that would allow her time for childcare:

> (Wave One) '[The] ideal world I maybe strive for is that at some point I can balance that by working around the hours of them being at school. So they're at school, I work, they're off school, I care for them … I don't want to have to call on childcare.'

> (Wave Two) 'I want to be the one who looks after my children. I don't want to have to have someone else. That's always been my thing.' (Louise, single mother, two children aged 9 and 7)

The overall lack of change in the participants' work–care choices over time raises questions about the aim of Universal Credit to change behaviours and attitudes to paid work (see Chapter Three). The government has contended that policy levers within Universal Credit (including intensified conditionality) will lead to changes in claimants' attitudes and behaviours regarding paid work and ultimately result in improved labour market outcomes (DWP, 2017b). However, this study suggests that for primary carers of children, the conditionality within Universal Credit does not change attitudes to paid work, and that there is a failure to recognise the strength of mothers' moral considerations about what is right for their children in relation to their engagement in unpaid care and paid work (Barlow et al, 2002).

Extent to which the Claimant Commitments were negotiated

This section explores the extent to which the participants were able to negotiate their Claimant Commitments. Claimants need to accept a Claimant Commitment to receive Universal Credit payments. According to the government literature, the Claimant Commitment is a 'contract' between the claimant and the state (DWP, 2014a) which sets out what claimants have 'agreed' to do to prepare for and look for work or increase their earnings (DWP, 2020b). However, for the most part, the participants had no choice in their Claimant Commitments and felt compelled to accept them as they knew that if they did not, they would not receive Universal Credit payments. Of the 24 mothers, 20 explained there had been no negotiation when their commitments were set (see also Fawcett Society, 2015; Dwyer, 2018a), and the 4 participants who did consider that their commitments had been negotiated all had easements. 'Lucy' explained that there was a lack of negotiation when her Claimant Commitment was drawn up, and later in the interview, she showed her frustration at being subject to potential sanction when she did not consider that her work-related requirements were appropriate in the first place:

> 'I don't think that it was [negotiated]. … I think it was as though there were a variety of different kind of holes that you can sort of fit in, and they sort of allocated you to one and it was either that or actually you don't fit any of them so you wouldn't be entitled to anything. … You can be penalised if you're not fulfilling the requirements that perhaps weren't actually the true requirements at the time, it was just that it was slotted in because it seemed the least worst route to take under the different options that you could go for with Universal Credit.' (Lucy, single mother, two children aged 8 and 6, wave one)

Several mothers reported they had not had any discussion about the Claimant Commitment, and therefore had no opportunity to negotiate their work-related requirements. At other times, the participants' attempts to negotiate their Claimant Commitments did not result in alterations or accommodations. As Michelle was already working 16 to 20 hours as a self-employed cleaner, she initially objected to having to agree to look for more work. However, she was told to agree to her work-related requirements regardless:

> 'When I spoke to the work coach, I said, "I don't really need to be looking for work do I, cos I am working?" And they was like, "Oh yeah, yeah, just agree." So I just did.' (Michelle, single mother, two children aged 9 and 7, wave one)

The general lack of negotiation of the Claimant Commitment raises questions as to the description of this document as a 'contract' and the use of the word 'agree' in the government literature (DWP, 2014a, 2020b). This language implies claimants have choice as to whether or not they commit to carrying out their work-related requirements (Dwyer and Ellison, 2009b). However, the participants were made very aware that if they did not accept their Claimant Commitments, they would not get their Universal Credit payments. Therefore, as claimants need Universal Credit payments and can only get them if they accept their Claimant Commitments, the element of choice is missing and instead the Commitments are accepted under duress (Goodin, 2001; Dwyer and Ellison, 2009b; Standing, 2011). These findings are particularly concerning given that for half of the mothers in the study, the work-related requirements stated on their Claimant Commitments were incompatible with their work–care choices.

Experiences of compulsion over time

As noted in Chapter Four, in addition to work coaches having a role in setting work-related requirements, they are also largely responsible for implementing conditionality on an ongoing basis, and therefore their actions were important to the mothers' experiences of compulsion over time. For the study's participants, there was variation in the extent to which the requirements were enforced by work coaches on an ongoing basis. This was particularly evident in the mothers' reflections on the work coaches' differing expectations and monitoring of claimants' reporting of mandatory work-related activity on their online journals. Some mothers were asked to do a considerable amount of reporting, and this was checked up on:

> 'I had to show that I was looking for work and I had to write on this journal every single day pretty much what I'd done, whether I'd looked in newspapers an' every kind of, anything that I could to prove that I was looking for work. And if you didn't, you'd get like: "You know there's nothing been on your journal for a while. What's going on?"' (Nicola, single mother, three children aged 18, 16 and 9, wave one)

This experience greatly contrasts with that of Kirsty, who explained:

> 'When I go in, she's [work coach] not saying, you know, let me have a look at what you've done.' (Kirsty, single mother, two children aged 7 and 5, wave one)

Kirsty had an easement based on her housing situation (see Chapter Four), and other mothers with easements also typically considered they faced more understanding and leniency from their work coaches in regard to mandatory work-related requirements.

While some of the variation in experiences can be explained through the presence of an easement and the different employment status of the participants (discussed later), there was variation in the way the work coaches set and monitored work-related requirements on an ongoing basis which cannot be explained entirely by differences within the sample. The findings suggest that discretion on the part of frontline workers was also significant to the mothers' experiences of conditionality. This demonstrates the influence frontline workers can have on the delivery of government policy (Lipsky, 2010) and also supports claims that frontline workers are important specifically to the delivery of conditionality policies (Fletcher, 2011; Nothdurfter, 2016; Caswell et al, 2017). Concerns have been raised that increased discretion may result in inconsistency in referrals for sanctions (National Audit Office, 2016) and leave single parents vulnerable to subjective decisions at crucial junctures of their claim (Cain, 2016). This study shows that there can be considerable inconsistencies even in the more routine aspects of how conditionality is enforced.

Over time, all of the participants (apart from one who had a fit note) who were unemployed at the second wave of interviews reported that there had been an increase in mandatory requirements between the two waves of interviews. This included directives to apply for particular jobs, to undertake mandatory training and to attend job fairs. 'Danielle' explained that over time, there had been an increase in the mandatory requirements she was expected to meet. The forthcoming quotes show the mandatory activities she was required to fulfil in addition to her weekly job search hours and work search review appointments at the two waves of interviews:

> (Wave One) 'I've got an appointment today to go over my CV and start on the handing out, and my appointment last week just happened to be on the same day as a job fair so I got sent along to the job fair as well.'

> (Wave Two) 'There was the [mandatory training at a retailer] thing and I was being asked to apply for specific jobs as well and being given sheets for them, and they wanted feedback that I'd definitely done it.' (Danielle, single mother, two children aged 8 and 7)

Crucially, this increase in mandatory requirements was not accompanied by an increase in support for obtaining paid work (see Chapter Five). This indicates that the work coach's response to ongoing unemployment was to increase compulsion rather than help claimants address barriers to paid work.

The participants who were self-employed had different experiences of compulsion over time, related to their employment status. In the first wave of interviews, the self-employed mothers generally experienced lighter conditionality than the mothers who were required to job search. For example, they were required to attend fewer work coach meetings and could not be subject to directives to apply for particular jobs. 'Nicola', who experienced a lot of monitoring from her work coach, explained that she became self-employed to avoid certain requirements:

> 'I used to be a self-employed hairdresser, so I thought well that's probably my best option now, cos he [work coach] basically said, you know, you need to, if a job comes up at Aldi in [village], you have to take it, and it wouldn't, they wouldn't take the hours into consideration.' (Nicola, single mother, three children aged 18, 16 and 9, wave one)

Most of the mothers had, or were working towards, university-level qualifications. This suggests that more-educated mothers in receipt of Universal Credit can use their cultural and social capital (Bourdieu, 1986) to become self-employed and subsequently reduce the levels of compulsion they are subject to, particularly during the first year of their claim (the start-up period). However, in the second wave of interviews, as the self-employed participants were subject to the MIF (see Chapter Three), these participants were under increased pressure to meet their expected earnings. The following quotes illustrate this change in pressure:

> (Wave One) 'They seem to be very hands-off at the moment. … Because they [the work-related requirements] weren't defined, then it's as I see fit, in a way.'

> (Wave Two) 'I think it's very difficult with the self-employed and the Minimum Income Floor. … I think … the sort of stress around it for me comes from the fluctuation [in earnings].' (Lucy, single mother, two children aged 9 and 7)

Whereas the unemployed claimants were subject to potential sanction for failing to undertake work-related requirements, the self-employed claimants were certain to incur reductions in overall income if they did not meet the MIF. Therefore, arguably, conditionality was more strictly enforced for these mothers in regard to reaching a certain level of earnings.

The mothers who were subject to in-work conditionality generally faced lesser compulsion than those who were unemployed; however, there was considerable variation in the experiences of these mothers. In the first wave of interviews, two of the mothers subject to in-work conditionality did not have any regular contact with their work coaches, whereas the other two mothers had to take part in telephone appointments in which they were asked about their attempts to find more paid work or increase their earnings. In the second wave of interviews, the telephone appointments ceased for one of the mothers despite only a very slight increase in her earnings. However, in Leanne's case, compulsion increased. She frequently had to attend both in-person and telephone appointments, and report her job search activity on her online journal. She explained at the two waves of interviews:

> (Wave One) 'So "To-do list" [on her online Universal Credit account], and it says take part in your work search review by phone. That's the only thing I've got to do.'

> (Wave Two) 'If you're not working 25 hours – which is why I'm hating Universal Credit – you have to nonstop go to interviews or they're messaging you for interviews or they're on the phone to make sure you're keeping up with your Commitments … you've got this fricking

> machine, this Universal Credit bloody bully that literally is on you all the time.' (Leanne, single mother, three children aged 13, 10 and 5)

Leanne was working 16 hours a week and should not have been subject to job search requirements as her earnings were above the AET (see Chapter Three). This suggests that the variation in experiences of the employed participants may be due partly to different work coaches' knowledge of the relevant legislation regarding in-work conditionality (Woudheysen, 2019).

Across the sample, one common finding was the lack of application of sanctions for noncompliance with mandatory work-related requirements. One mother in paid work thought she may have been sanctioned for not completing mandatory online administrative tasks, but she was not sure as her Universal Credit payments routinely fluctuated. Over the course of the study, four of the mothers missed appointments with their work coaches. While these mothers were warned this could result in a sanction, their reasons for missing the appointments were accepted and they were not referred for a sanction. However, in Anna's case, following this incident her work coach told her she needed to update her journal more:

> 'But the next time I went to see him, he was like, "Look at this, your journal, you haven't updated your journal," and I didn't really register when he said … I thought it was just for fun. It's not just for fun.' (Anna, single mother, one child aged 4, wave one)

Similarly, Jamila who had not followed a directive to apply for a particular job (because she did not have a CV) was not sanctioned but was told that she had ten days to follow her work coach's directives or face sanction:

> 'And last time they was send me for ten days if I will not do what they told me, and that was difficult for me

> cos they told me about checking everything, changing something like that and looking for a job. Now was pressing me cos I have to do it before ten days. Now on, I was worry they can cut my money.' (Jamila, single mother, two children aged 8 and 5, wave two)

Therefore, noncompliance with mandatory work-related requirements resulted in increased monitoring and threats of sanction but did not result in referrals for sanctions. There are several possible reasons for this. First, at the time of the field work, Universal Credit sanction rates in the UK had considerably decreased after peaking in early 2017 (Webster, 2019). Second, there may have been leniency towards those who did not comply with requirements on account of the fact they were mothers. The majority of the participants who missed their appointments did so due to their caring responsibilities – for example, one mother missed a telephone appointment as she was dropping her children off at school and did not hear her phone. This suggests that mothers' caring responsibilities may be taken into account when the potential for sanctions arises (see Chapter Four). Third, four out of the five participants who missed appointments had, or previously had, an easement, and this may also have impacted the leniency they received. Fourth, and possibly related to the fact they had an easement (see Chapter Five), the majority of those who missed appointments had particularly positive relationships with their work coaches, and so their work coaches may have been reluctant to sanction them. This highlights the complex and dual role work coaches have of both providing employment support to claimants and enforcing a conditionality regime (Fletcher, 2011; Patrick, 2017).

Despite the variations in the levels and monitoring of work-related requirements on an ongoing basis and the lack of sanctions, the overwhelming majority of the mothers reported experiencing pressure from the Universal Credit system. The following quotes indicate that this pressure was caused by the expectation to enter paid work, the mandatory work-related requirements and the fear of sanctions (discussed later):

> 'I know it's only ten hours, but still it's like I just think, oh, what have I done this week? Or if I've not been to [women's charity] or I've not seen [single-parent keyworker], it's like, oh, yes, let's just knuckle down and look at some jobs now and just say what you've been looking at and yeah … so sometimes there is that pressure.' (Helen, single mother, two children aged 13 and 11, wave two)

> 'I think there's pressure on being a mum anyway and then pressure to work and pressure to find a job and worry about sanctions.' (Laura, single mother, one child aged 2, wave one)

The mothers spoke of the pressure in negative terms, with some commenting that it was unnecessary and detrimental:

> 'Yeah pressure. It wasn't a nice feeling. It made you feel quite low to be honest.' (Jessica, single mother, two children aged 6 and 4, wave one)

Such punitive and paternalistic compulsion within conditionality policies may contribute to a weakening of self-esteem and therefore undermine claimants' ability to find paid work (Wright and Patrick, 2019).

Overall, the analysis shows that the participants were subject to differing levels and types of compulsion. This varied by easement (particularly in the first wave of interviews), work coach discretion and employment status. The longitudinal analysis shows that for many participants, the compulsion increased over time. The participants who were unemployed throughout the course of the study faced the highest levels of directives and monitoring over time in regard to ongoing work-related requirements. While this latter finding is unsurprising, it is problematic given that these participants tended to have health conditions, previous experiences of domestic abuse and lower levels of cultural and social capital, yet were not given additional support. The analysis also shows that work coach discretion is important to participants' experiences of the conditionality within Universal Credit. However, there are limits to the impacts work coach discretion has on the amount of compulsion which the participants feel they are under due to the mandatory expectation within the system, backed by sanctions, that they will search for and undertake paid work. As a result, despite the participants being subject to varying expectations and monitoring, most of them experienced considerable levels of pressure within the Universal Credit system.

Views on the compulsion within Universal Credit

Through exploring the mothers' views on conditionality, this section further illuminates the extent to which they experienced compulsion within the Universal Credit system and also provides context for their responses to the compulsion discussed in the preceding section. This section highlights the mothers' resentment at being subject to conditionality and also the mismatch between the compulsion within Universal Credit and the mothers' views regarding the amount of agency they should be afforded in relation to their engagement in paid work and unpaid care.

Views on choice in the Universal Credit system

In line with feminist arguments emphasising the importance of promoting genuine choice in regard to engagement in unpaid care and paid work (Lewis, 1997), the majority of the participants considered mothers' ability to exercise choice as important (see also Judge, 2015). Most of the participants expressed the view that mothers should have choice as to when they enter paid work and how much paid work they do. When expressing their views on the amount of choice mothers should have regarding their engagement in paid work, many participants made negative comparisons with the compulsion in the Universal Credit system:

> 'As a parent … it's your choice whether you want to work or stay at home and look after your children, you know. And to be now put under the pressure with this Universal Credit, you know, is really unfair.' (Nicola, single mother, three children aged 18, 16 and 10, wave two)

Indeed, many of the mothers expressed the view that there is a lack of choice within the Universal Credit system:

> 'There's no choice, there's no element of choice – would you rather look after the children or would you rather work? Nobody ever asks that question.' (Lucy, single mother, two children aged 8 and 6, wave one)

The vast majority of the participants resented being subject to work-related requirements. There were three main objections to this. Some participants thought the requirements were too extensive given their caring responsibilities, some resented the control imposed on them, and some felt that the requirements were unfair (particularly in light of factors outside of their control, such as health conditions and the availability of jobs:

> 'It really annoyed me to be fair, I'm not going to lie, because that's hours in the day that I don't really have.' (Kirsty, single mother, two children aged 7 and 5, wave two)

> 'It feels restrictive and it feels very sort of top-down rather than sort of person centred, I supposed. Erm, a little bit

> sort of patriarchal maybe, sort of we know we know better you know.' (Lucy, single mother, two children aged 9 and 7, wave two)

> 'I was frantic, horrified and panicked that it was given to me, cos I … had a fit note, so I'd've thought that it should not have been given to me.' (Anna, single mother, one child aged 4, wave two)

These perceptions concerning lack of choice within the Universal Credit conditionality regime regarding mandatory engagement in paid work and work-related requirements, and the objections to the compulsion, support claims that this policy reduces mothers' choice about their engagement in unpaid care and paid work (Grabham and Smith, 2010; Davies, 2012, 2015; Whitworth and Griggs, 2013; Rafferty and Wiggan, 2017; Millar, 2019). This finding is significant given that a key aspect of exercising agency is the capacity for free choice (Gould, 1983; Lister, 2003; Wright, 2012; McNay, 2016), and enlarging women's capacity to exercise agency in regard to engagement in unpaid care and paid work is an essential element of creating a more gender-inclusive citizenship framework. This analysis also reflects the view that the aim within welfare-to-work policies should be to facilitate rather than compel mothers into paid work, given that they are often best placed to understand the appropriate number of paid work hours in light of their families' circumstances (Judge, 2015; Rafferty and Wiggan, 2017).

Views on sanctioning mothers

Across the sample, there was a lack of support for sanctioning mothers. The vast majority of the participants expressed the view that mothers should not be sanctioned. The main reasons for this centred on the participants' caring responsibilities. A common concern was the fact that sanctions would affect children, who would be negatively impacted through no fault of their own (see also Johnsen and Blenkinsopp, 2018):

> 'I mean, goodness me, we've got children to provide for. You're talking about taking money away from … you know, you're blaming. I mean, say, for example, yes you've got a mum who doesn't want to work and doesn't do any job search, you're penalising her children for that.' (Jessica, single mother, two children aged 6 and 4, wave one)

Another key reason for the view that mothers should not be sanctioned was that mothers are already carrying out an important role caring for their children:

> 'They are mothering. They're caring for their children. They are making sure that the home is well managed and that, you know, the food is being prepared and that their family is being cared for. That is their job. So definitely, why should, why would they be sanctioned? They shouldn't be sanctioned for doing their job.' (Christina, coupled mother, two children aged 15 and 6, wave one)

Also, among the mothers with experience of a joint claim, there was a lack of support for the way sanctioning operates in couples. All of them objected to the fact that if their partner did not comply with requirements, the whole family would be negatively affected due to the payment into one account:

> 'That shouldn't be like that. Yeah why should both people get sanctioned? Why should we be like … cos then that would be taking the money away from me and the children if [partner] can't attend one of his appointments? Why should we get sanctioned?' (Kelly, coupled mother, two children aged 4 and 2, wave one)

As also evidenced in Chapter Five, this illustrates one gendered issue of the joint claim wherein, regardless of whether the mother receives the Universal Credit payment, she can be subject to a loss of income if her partner does not comply with requirements and receives a sanction.

Overall, the views of the participants presented in this section combined with the experiences discussed in the two previous sections show that most of the participants were subject to a considerable degree of compulsion and objected to this. Particularly in light of the lack of choice the participants felt they had within the Universal Credit system, the analysis furthers concerns about the lack of agency afforded to mothers within the Universal Credit conditionality regime (Whitworth and Griggs, 2013). This finding corresponds with previous research which found that subjecting claimants to conditionality resulted in loss of agency (Wright and Patrick, 2019). The current study shows that in the context of families, there is a gendered dimension to this curtailment of agency. Across the sample, whether in a couple relationship or not, the mothers were more likely than the fathers to be subject to the compulsion within the Universal Credit system (as the mothers were disproportionately responsible for unpaid care, they were less likely to be in paid work). This once again demonstrates a lack of recognition of women's disproportionate responsibility for unpaid care and has the gendered outcome of subjecting women, who have historically been denied agency (McNay, 2016), to increasing amounts of surveillance and coercion.

Responses over time to the compulsion within Universal Credit

As social security claimants are not simply powerless victims, but can and do exercise agency (Finn, 2018; Wright et al, 2020), this section explores the extent to which, and ways in which, the mothers responded to the attempts from the Universal Credit system to dominate their agency in relation to engagement in mandatory work-related activities and paid work. The mothers responded in differing ways to the compulsion within Universal Credit. Three main responses were evident in the findings, and some of the mothers exhibited more than one of these responses.

The predominant response was to conscientiously comply with the work-related requirements. The vast majority of the participants carried out their work-related requirements (and at times went beyond what was expected of them):

> 'I've been doing basically everything they're … asking me to do. Even when like I was ill, I went in cos I was worried about not getting my money.' (Nicola, single mother, three children aged 18, 16 and 9, wave one)

As this comment indicates, the mothers complied to avoid a sanction. In line with previous research (Dwyer, 2018b; Wright and Patrick, 2019), the fear of being sanctioned was very prevalent across the sample:

> 'There's just this constant kind of anxiety because you don't want to be sanctioned.' (Christina, coupled mother, two children aged 15 and 6, wave one)

For some participants, the fear of a sanction may have come from their interactions with their work coaches, previously discussed. The participants' fear may also have come from the government literature they received. As Leanne explained, the Claimant Commitment heavily emphasised the potential for sanctions:

> 'It's sanctions, sanctions, sanctions all over this bloody thing.' (Leanne, single mother, three children aged 12, 10 and 5, wave one)

Some of the participants (including some who were in paid work) were frequently required to accept their Claimant

Commitments (despite lack of changes to these). Additionally, some of the participants were sent reminders about sanctions and were repeatedly required to read about sanctions (under the threat of sanction for failure to do so) in their online Universal Credit journal. These findings, which show that the emphasis on sanctions in the government literature led to fear of sanction and ultimately compliance – despite the lack of referrals for sanctions – reinforce claims that conditionality attempts to discipline and coerce claimants into fulfilling work-related requirements by instilling fear (Wright and Patrick, 2019; Wright et al, 2020).

This analysis corresponds with that from a study investigating the lived experiences of conditionality in Ireland, which found that it is the threat of sanction – rather than sanctions themselves – that is used as a mechanism to ensure compliance with work-related requirements (Finn, 2020). The current study shows there is a gendered dimension to the use of the threat of sanction to ensure compliance. Many of the mothers were particularly keen to avoid a sanction because they had either the sole responsibility or the vast majority of the responsibility for ensuring their children's material needs were met and were very concerned about the negative impacts of potential sanctions on their children. This indicates that within Universal Credit, there is a failure to recognise not only mothers' main responsibilities for unpaid caring and domestic labour, but also their role as the main managers of poverty (Lister, 2004), as the fear of sanctions can be particularly pernicious for those with caring responsibilities and results in adverse gendered impacts such as stress and anxiety (see Chapter Four).

A second response to the compulsion within Universal Credit, evident for five of the mothers, was for mothers to make it appear that they were fully complying with job search requirements – for example, by applying for jobs they knew they would not get and reporting job search activities they had not undertaken. One of the mothers described recording her job search activity in her work journal:

> 'I'm … there trying to present myself on my work journal as being this really productive person. I was trying to organise a litter pick and doing these other projects which I can't even remember now, but, you know, I was trying to get involved and appear like I was doing something, without doing anything.' (Anna, single mother, one child aged 4, wave one)

A third response, evident for three of the mothers, was to overtly not comply with the majority of the work-related requirements. While these mothers did attend mandatory appointments with their work coaches, they did not carry out their job search requirements. For 'Jodie', this was because she had a newly diagnosed health condition (but had not received an updated Claimant Commitment that took this into account):

> 'I haven't spoken to anybody about it. I'm not doing it.' (Jodie, coupled mother, one child aged 5, wave one)

Jamila did not comply with her work-related requirements because she prioritised the care of her children (see Chapter Four):

> 'It's difficult to me, honestly, because I have children. I have to look after them. They need me, I need them.' (Jamila, single mother, two children aged 7 and 5)

The longitudinal analysis shows that over time, there was little change in how the participants responded to the compulsion within Universal Credit. The main response was conscientious compliance followed by apparent compliance. The forthcoming comments illustrate the consistency of the participants' responses:

> (Wave One) 'I want to just follow the rules of what I'm meant to be doing and, obviously, ideally just be self-sufficient and make enough money anyway.'

> (Wave Two) 'I just want to follow the rules that are already set out and just, yeah, not cause any, like, attention to myself.' (Jennifer, single mother, two children aged 6 and 3)

Two of the participants who did not comply with work-related requirements in the first wave of interviews did not take part in a second interview, and therefore their responses over time were not documented. Jamila, who did not comply previously, on account of her caring responsibilities, did comply more at the second wave of interviews. This was due to the increased threat of sanction that she experienced after she had not followed a directive to apply for a particular job, mentioned earlier:

> 'Now on, I was worry they can cut my money, and I find now on, finally I get something and writing everything they told me to do, I do it.' (Jamila, single mother, two children aged 8 and 5, wave two)

However, while Jamila was complying with mandatory work-related requirements at the second wave of interviews, she still did not want a job, as she continued to prioritise her caring responsibilities. On being asked if she would try to get a job, she answered:

> 'When my children grown up [and] I have someone to help me at home, I can look. But if I don't have someone to help me at home, I can't do it. I need my certificates first. Improve my English, learn my children the best way.' (Jamila, single mother, two children aged 8 and 5, wave two)

Research conducted by NatCen for the DWP (2017b) also found that while the conditionality within Universal Credit drove compliance among claimants, at times this was not productive. Therefore, there are indications that while the compulsion within Universal Credit can change claimants' job search behaviour, it does not always lead to concerted efforts to obtain paid work if claimants do not want to undertake paid work, or more paid work, at the current time. This suggests the theory of change behind Universal Credit (see Chapter Three) has considerable limitations. More broadly, this indicates there are limits to the influence behaviouristic policies such as conditionality can exert and, therefore, also limits to the extent they can achieve their intended outcomes.

Overall, the findings show that the main response to the compulsion within Universal Credit is conscientious compliance. Previous research has shown that while demonstrating a variety of responses to conditionality, claimants' predominant response is acquiescence (Wright et al, 2020). In the current study, this response was due to fear of sanction, perpetuated in part by the emphasis on sanctions in the Claimant Commitments and other government literature. This fear was exacerbated by the mothers' responsibilities for ensuring their children's material needs were met. The findings also demonstrate that some participants used their agency to maintain their work–care choices by appearing to comply, or not complying, with work-related requirements. Prior research has similarly found that despite the considerable constraints of welfare conditionality policies, claimants can and do act according to their own interests (Finn, 2018). The data is limited over time concerning the participants who overtly did not comply with requirements. However, there are suggestions that as none of the participants were overtly engaged in noncompliance at the second wave of interviews, perhaps due to the increased compulsion faced by those who did not comply, such resistance was hard to maintain. While this may have meant that these participants' agency was dominated in regard to carrying out work-related requirements, some still used their agency to resist the overall requirement to enter paid work. These outcomes are discussed further in the next section.

Overall impacts on participants' agency

The compulsion within the Universal Credit conditionality regime and the mothers' responses to this had impacts on the mothers' agency in regard to engagement in work-related requirements and paid work. In terms of the work-related requirements, for the vast majority of the participants, being subject to the conditionality within Universal Credit resulted in them engaging in activities that they would not have otherwise chosen to do. These activities included attending appointments at the JCP, carrying out extensive online job search, reporting job search activity on their Universal Credit journals, applying for jobs they could not do, taking part in mandatory training activities and fulfilling online administration and tasks. Zoe commented:

> 'I don't want to waste time applying for jobs I'm not going to do or have a job that I don't want to do when I could be finding or getting the actual job that I would stay in for the foreseeable future.' (Zoe, single mother, two children aged 14 and 6, wave one)

As this comment shows, a main reason why the participants did not choose to engage in their work-related requirements from their own volition was that they did not think they were helpful, or thought they were counterproductive, in moving them into paid work (see also Patrick, 2017). As explained previously, those who were unemployed and subject to job search requirements had more directives and monitoring and therefore were particularly likely to have to engage in such activities against their choice.

More broadly, the conditionality within Universal Credit and the mothers' responses to it had varying impacts on the mothers' agency in relation to their engagement in paid work and unpaid care. As explored previously, some of the mothers resisted the compulsion within Universal Credit and avoided entering paid work (or increasing their paid work hours). Additionally, five of the mothers who entered paid work since the start of their Universal Credit claim had wanted to start paid work immediately and obtained jobs in line with their work–care choices, in terms of work hours and type of work. As there was alignment between the paid work expectations of Universal Credit and these mothers' choices, their agency was not dominated. Emily explained:

> 'I am lucky in that I have never felt that I'm being made to do something that I don't want to do. … I've never been forced into situations by the benefit system that meant that I felt they were making me work when I'd rather be with my son.' (Emily, single mother, one child aged 8, wave two)

However, partly as a result of the compulsion within Universal Credit, four of the mothers entered paid work sooner than they wanted to. For three of these participants, this went against their preferences for undertaking unpaid care, and for one, it conflicted with her caring responsibilities and her studies. Although Kirsty had a work coach who was understanding of her caring responsibilities and did not monitor her job search activity, she still perceived that she was compelled into paid work before she was ready:

> 'I think if it was my choice, then I probably would have waited a little bit longer just so that … cos I'm stressed a lot and my kids see that so, yeah, I probably just maybe would [have] waited a little bit longer.' (Kirsty, single mother, two children aged 7 and 5, wave two)

Paid work requirements also affected the mothers' agency in regard to engagement in paid work in other ways. Due to the compulsion within Universal Credit, three of the mothers were working longer hours than they wanted to given their caring responsibilities, one had to change from self-employment to employment against her choice, and one entered a low-level job rather than take her time to obtain a job that would help her establish her career. It also routinely constrained the mothers' ability to pursue their long-term career aspirations (see Chapter Five).

Overall, for some mothers, the work-related expectations of Universal Credit aligned with their work–care choices and, therefore, did not dominate their agency, and others used their agency to resist engagement in paid work (or increased engagement in paid work). However, for others, the outcome of the policy was engagement in paid work that went against their choices, particularly in terms of when they entered paid work and how much paid work they undertook. Significantly, for the majority of these mothers, their employment outcomes conflicted with their commitment to unpaid care. This confirms concerns regarding the potential for compulsion to force mothers to do what they consider to be morally wrong (Barlow et al, 2002). This study also shows that rather than establishing the right to care so citizens can have genuine choice about their engagement in unpaid care (Knijn and Kremer, 1997), this policy denies some women the choice to care.

Conclusion

The analysis presented in this chapter shows that typically, mothers experience a considerable amount of compulsion within the Universal Credit conditionality regime. The participants' Claimant Commitments were on the whole imposed rather than negotiated. While the participants were subject to varying degrees of directives and monitoring from their work coaches, other aspects of the conditionality regime, such as the threat of sanction, resulted in the participants feeling subject to considerable pressure and perceiving that they lacked choice in regard to engagement in unpaid care and paid work. There was some variation across the sample in that those with easements generally faced less stringent compulsion initially; however, as they tended to remain unemployed (see Chapter Five), they were often subject to prolonged and increased compulsion over time. Those with the least amount of cultural and social capital and who were furthest from the paid labour market experienced the greatest amount of intrusion regarding routine work-related requirements. The mothers with higher levels of cultural and social capital were subject to fewer directives and less scrutiny, particularly in the first year of their claim, due to their self-employed status. However, being subject to the MIF after a start-up period resulted in a considerable amount of compulsion regarding the level of earnings they reached. The findings also suggest that in differing ways, compulsion increased over time across the sample. Most of the mothers responded to the compulsion by complying with work-related requirements; however, others resisted the compulsion through apparent compliance, overt noncompliance or nonproductive compliance.

The analysis also shows the conditionality within Universal Credit has wider implications for women's relationship to the social security system and for their citizenship status. The study demonstrates that the conditionality limits women's ability to exercise choice and reduces their control over their daily lives, mainly in relation to carrying out work-related requirements but also in terms of their engagement in unpaid care and paid work. It can deny women the choice to undertake unpaid care, and it also limits women's ability to pursue their chosen career aspirations. Therefore, rather than expand women's ability to exercise agency so that they can engage in unpaid care and participate in the paid labour market more fully in line with a gender-inclusive concept of citizenship, this policy further limits it. Consequently, this study strengthens claims that conditionality policies reinforce structures of subordination (Goodin, 2002) and shows that this occurs in relation to gender as women – who already face considerable constraints on their agency – are subject to patriarchal control from the state.

SEVEN

Conclusion

Introduction

The introduction of Universal Credit in the UK entails the most intensive and extensive application of conditionality to date (Dwyer and Wright, 2014; Wright and Dwyer, 2022). As women are particularly affected by the new conditionality regime for lead carers of children, investigation into how women experience and view this policy was essential. This book has reported on research that explored over time the impacts of the new conditionality regime for lead carers on the valuing of unpaid care, women's position in the paid labour market and women's agency in relation to engagement in unpaid care and paid work.

This concluding chapter starts by highlighting the key findings. It then discusses the implications of the conditionality within Universal Credit for women's citizenship and the social security system, and explains how the social security system can be changed to promote a more gender-inclusive citizenship framework. It gives specific recommendations for the conditionality within Universal Credit. The chapter ends by articulating how the conditionality within Universal Credit furthers an androcentric concept of citizenship and highlighting the importance of seeking and incorporating the views of claimants when devising welfare reform.

Effects on mothers' caring roles and responsibilities, employment trajectories and agency

The research shows that within Universal Credit policy and practice, there is an almost exclusive emphasis on paid work and a routine failure to recognise and take into account mothers' caring responsibilities (see Chapter Four). As a result, mandatory expectations of work-related requirements and paid work hinder mothers' ability to deliver unpaid care by limiting time to undertake unpaid care and increasing tensions in interactions with children. The longitudinal analysis shows that these impacts are sustained over time and are often exacerbated by entrance into paid work. There are also considerable challenges in taking children to appointments at the JCP. This also undermines mothers' caring responsibilities and roles. Additionally, there were indications that the conditionality erodes mothers' caring identities as some of the participants experienced shame and stigma on account of undertaking unpaid care. This emphasis on paid work to the detriment of unpaid care and caring identities devalues unpaid care.

The longitudinal analysis shows that the conditionality within Universal Credit has limited positive impacts on mothers' employment trajectories. A significant proportion of the participants did not enter paid work and there was a distinct lack of progression in the paid labour market over time (see Chapter Five). While some of the participants had moved into paid work since the start of their Universal Credit claim, they were more likely to attribute this to their own motivation and efforts rather than the conditionality within Universal Credit. Furthermore, the majority of these participants entered gendered, low-paid, insecure, part-time work, regardless of education level, and some did not sustain paid work. This suggests that the Universal Credit conditionality regime does not support women in obtaining jobs that improve their disadvantaged position in the paid labour market. There were also indications that the work first approach inherent within the Universal Credit regime furthers women's disadvantaged labour market position as it resulted in some mothers taking the first job available, regardless of compatibility with education, experience and caring responsibilities, and limited some of the mothers' opportunities for long-term career planning and training. Key factors contributing to the lack of sustained moves into secure, adequately paid work and the lack of increases in earnings were the severe difficulties in accessing the formal childcare provision within Universal Credit and the absence of substantive employment-related support from work coaches and the JCP.

The research demonstrates that mothers experienced a considerable amount of compulsion within the Universal Credit conditionality regime (see Chapter Six). While some participants resisted this compulsion, the majority complied with work-related requirements. The compulsion was particularly evident in the lack of negotiation when the Claimant Commitment was formed and in the mandatory requirement to undertake paid work or increase earnings backed by sanctions and the MIF. For some participants, interactions with work coaches added to the compulsion they experienced. The longitudinal analysis shows that the amount of compulsion the participants experienced increased over time across the sample and indicated that subsequently, resistance to compulsion is difficult to maintain. Overall, the conditionality within Universal Credit limits women's ability to exercise agency in regard to engagement in work-related requirements, unpaid care and paid work, and in particular, it denies mothers the choice to undertake unpaid care.

While the analysis gives the overall experiences and views of the mothers within the sample, there was some notable variation in experiences, primarily according to whether the participants had an easement. The mothers with easements reported positive experiences in regard to some aspects of their Universal Credit claim; however, there was variation in the effects of these positive experiences on overall outcomes.

The mothers with easements were more likely to report that their caring responsibilities had been taken into account when work-related requirements were set by their work coaches and on an ongoing basis (see Chapter Four). Consequently, they were among the minority of mothers who did not think their caring responsibilities had been negatively impacted by their work-related requirements at the first wave of interviews. The mothers with easements were also more likely to have positive relationships with their work coaches (see Chapter Five). However, investigating employment outcomes over time showed that the mothers who either currently or previously had an easement were less likely to obtain paid work. Additionally, while the mothers with easements tended to report that the Claimant Commitment had been negotiated and that they received more leniency and understanding regarding ongoing enforcement of work-related requirements, they still felt that they were under an objectionable degree of compulsion within the Universal Credit conditionality regime and resented being subject to mandatory work-related requirements (see Chapter Six).

The role of the participants' work coaches was also important to the participants' experiences of and views on the Universal Credit conditionality regime. Across the sample, there was variation in the extent to which caring responsibilities were taken into account during ongoing interactions with work coaches (see Chapter Four), there were differences in the relationships with work coaches (see Chapter Five) and there were disparities in how, and the extent to which, the participants' work-related requirements were enforced on an ongoing basis by their work coaches (see Chapter Six). However, for the most part, the discretion of the work coaches had a limited impact on the overall experiences and views of the mothers, as other elements of the system significantly influenced how the mothers were affected by the conditionality within Universal Credit. For example, while some of the work coaches did not enforce work-related requirements, most of the participants experienced considerable levels of pressure within the Universal Credit system and perceived that they lacked choice in regard to engagement in unpaid care and paid work due to the overall sanction-backed expectation to enter paid work or increase earnings (see Chapter Six). Additionally, the study found that the work coaches did not use the extent of the discretion afforded to them (see Chapter Four). While the Universal Credit literature emphasises the role of the work coach in personalising work-related requirements (DWP, 2010c, 2011a), the research demonstrates that work-related requirements are not routinely tailored to caring responsibilities. This was problematic as it often resulted in work-related requirements that were incompatible with caring responsibilities and, therefore, difficult to fulfil. The next section turns to the broader implications of the Universal Credit conditionality regime.

Implications for the UK citizenship framework and social security system

This study has found that the conditionality within Universal Credit hinders attempts to create a gender-inclusive citizenship framework. Rather than increasing the recognition of unpaid care as a valid citizenship contribution, it further devalues it by promoting the gendered notion that paid work is the primary duty of citizenship. Whereas previously some (inferior) unconditional social rights were allocated based on caring responsibilities (see Chapter Two), citizenship is increasingly conceptualised in terms of duties (Skevik, 2005). By making mothers' access to social rights conditional on extended and intensified paid work-related behaviour, the conditionality within Universal Credit continues the erosion of the former recognition of unpaid care. This study confirms claims that activation policies introduce a shift in women's social citizenship, as they demand women's participation in the paid labour market as their citizenship contribution and neglect unpaid care (Skevik, 2005; Letablier et al, 2011). This is highly problematic given the social and economic value of unpaid care (see Chapter Two) and the value mothers attach to their unpaid caring roles, as evidenced in this study and others (for example, Duncan and Edwards, 1999; Gillies, 2007; Holloway and Pimlott-Wilson, 2016). Although mothers remain disproportionately responsible for unpaid care and are regularly left with the sole responsibility for this, the Universal Credit conditionality regime fails to recognise interdependency and devalues the necessary caring roles and responsibilities mothers carry out (see Chapter Four). Therefore, this conditionality furthers mothers' exclusion, reduces the recognition they receive for unpaid care, erodes their social identity and weakens their social positioning by diminishing their caring subjectivities (Kingfisher, 2002), rather than recognising and valuing unpaid care as an essential and valid citizenship contribution (see Chapters Two and Four).

While policies that seek to increase mothers' engagement in the paid labour market have the potential to increase their financial independence, and their recognition, social standing and access to social rights obtained through paid work, this study shows that the conditionality within Universal Credit does not help mothers acquire these. A key issue is the failure to address women's disproportionate responsibility for unpaid care, and at times the exacerbation of this (discussed later in relation to the joint claim). While there is an attempt within Universal Credit policy to achieve this through increasing help with formal childcare costs, this study shows the inadequacy of this measure and also the impossibility of completely commodifying care (see Chapters Four and Five). A second significant, and related, issue is the failure to help women overcome gender inequalities in the paid labour market. Instead, as this study shows, the Universal Credit conditionality regime is largely ineffective in helping mothers enter secure, sustainable, adequately paid jobs and progress in paid work, and can be detrimental to long-term job prospects through the emphasis on getting claimants into any paid work quickly (see Chapter Five). Conditionality thereby expects unemployed lead carers of children to participate in, and uphold, gender inequalities in the paid labour market (Edmiston, 2018). Therefore, current conditionality policy and practice demands women obtain their citizenship status on the same terms as men, through entering paid work, without recognising women's caring responsibilities and their different position in the paid labour market. Consequently, the conditionality within Universal Credit does not facilitate women's attempts to obtain full citizenship status in its current gendered form, and at times it impedes these through exacerbating gender inequalities in the paid labour market.

This study also shows that the conditionality within Universal Credit limits women's agency in regard to engagement in unpaid care and paid work (although some women resist this to an extent). Within Universal Credit policy, mothers are denied the choice to undertake unpaid care from when the youngest child is aged 3 (see Chapter Six). This contributes towards the failure to recognise and value women's unpaid caring contributions. The conditionality regime also denies mothers a certain amount of control over their paid work decisions – for example, by curtailing their pursuit of long-term career aspirations – which limits their ability to improve their position in the paid labour market, as previously discussed. These constraints placed on women's agency accelerate a notable shift in policy. There was a period of time prior to the late 1990s when the British social security system afforded women the choice (albeit a constrained one) between working and mothering (Letablier et al, 2011). However, policies implemented from New Labour's time in office onwards have increasingly compelled women to be paid workers (see Chapter Three), and this compulsion has culminated in the introduction of Universal Credit. Therefore, rather than enlarging women's agency to help create a recognition of unpaid care and to support women's participation in the paid labour market, the conditionality within Universal Credit limits women's agency and therefore inhibits a key means of creating a more gender-inclusive citizenship framework.

There are also specific implications of the conditionality within Universal Credit for the citizenship rights of coupled women. The joint claim involves a single payment into one bank account, and both members of a couple have to fulfil their work-related requirements to maintain the household's full entitlement to Universal Credit. As evidenced in this study, a mother can lose her entire entitlement to Universal Credit payments due to the actions of her partner (see Chapter Five). Therefore, the joint liability for fulfilling work-related requirements within the Universal Credit joint claim results in a weakening of social rights for coupled mothers, as their access to benefit payments is now conditional on not only their own behaviour but also that of their partners. This is particularly problematic given that women have more of the responsibility for ensuring their children's material needs are met (Sung and Bennett, 2007). As this study shows, an additional gendered outcome of this is that coupled women help fulfil their partners' work-related requirements (see Chapter Five). Therefore, within couples, Universal Credit policy can exacerbate the current gendered division of unpaid responsibilities within households to the detriment of women's levels of stress and tiredness, and their ability to participate in the paid labour market and, therefore, obtain citizenship status.

Of considerable concern, the negative impacts and implications of the conditionality within Universal Credit are only pertinent to mothers on low incomes. Mothers who do not need to claim Universal Credit due to the level of their own or their partners' earnings, or whose household earnings are consistently above the relevant CET (see Chapter Three), are exempt from work-related requirements. The conditionality within Universal Credit subsequently devalues the unpaid care carried out by mothers who are on the lowest incomes in society. These mothers are not deemed to be making a valid citizenship contribution, whereas wealthier mothers who look after their children full time do not receive the censure of 'irresponsible citizen' as they are considered self-sufficient by virtue of their partners' incomes. The study also indicates that the conditionality within Universal Credit weakens low-income women's position in the paid labour market, thereby adding to inequalities among women (see Chapter Two) and failing to help low-income women obtain citizenship status through paid work. Additionally, as Harrison and Sanders argue, there is a 'social division of social control' (2014, p 11) whereby governments apply the most coercive measures aimed at changing behaviour to the poorest members of society (see also Dwyer, 1998). This is evident within Universal Credit policy, as the coercion to enter paid work is only experienced by those on the lowest incomes and not by all mothers in society. Specifically regarding the choice to carry out unpaid care, the study reinforces concerns that welfare-to-work policies result in disparities of care whereby poor families are particularly denied the right to give unpaid care (Haylett, 2003). Therefore, this study contributes to claims that prevailing welfare-to-work policy 'risks positioning impoverished single mothers "under erasure", invisible as mothers or moral citizens, and visible only as low waged worker citizens' (Pulkingham et al, 2010, p 267) and shows that due to the introduction of Universal Credit, this also applies to low-income coupled mothers.

In demonstrating how the conditionality within Universal Credit hinders attempts to create a more gender-inclusive version of citizenship, this study highlights deficiencies in current gendered conceptions of citizenship. It shows the persistent difficulties low-income mothers have in obtaining full citizenship status on the same terms as men and the problems with sidelining unpaid care. Therefore, the findings from this study further the argument that citizenship needs to be reconceptualised to be inclusive of women (Pateman, 1989; Cass, 1994; Lister, 2003; Pascall, 2012). As demonstrated in this study, unpaid care is an essential and valuable contribution that entails hard work and non-commodifiable relational and affective aspects (see Chapter Four). Since engaging in unpaid care currently results in a reduction in citizenship status (Knijn and Kremer, 1997), citizenship needs to be redefined so that unpaid care is viewed as a valid citizenship contribution (Knijn and Kremer, 1997; Sevenhuijsen, 2000; Tronto, 2001; Pateman, 2005). Under this citizenship framework, carrying out unpaid care would accrue social rights and respect akin to paid employment (Fraser and Gordon, 1994; Pascall, 2012; Cantillon and Lynch, 2017). To help bring about a comprehensive valuing of unpaid care, the concept of the independent wage earner needs to be deconstructed and replaced with recognition of interdependency which highlights that everybody needs to give and receive unpaid care at some point in their lives (Knijn and Kremer, 1997; Sevenhuijsen, 2000; Lynch and Lyons, 2009). For unpaid care to be valued, policies that provide time to care and financial resources are needed (Williams, 2001; Lynch and Walsh, 2009; Cantillon and Lynch, 2017).

Establishing the value of unpaid care does not entail diminishing the importance of women's engagement in paid work, as within a gender-inclusive framework, this remains a key citizenship contribution (Knijn and Kremer, 1997). While participating in paid work can accrue financial rewards, for the mothers of this study, these gains were slight, confirming claims that merely inserting women into the paid labour market does not guarantee more gender-equal outcomes (Annesley et al, 2010). This study therefore shows that gender inequalities in the paid labour market and women's disproportionate responsibility for unpaid care need to be addressed so that there can be more parity between women (from across the sociodemographic spectrum) and men in terms of participating in, and obtaining the rewards from, paid work (Cass, 1994; Lister, 2003; Pascall, 2012). This includes implementing policies that contribute to combating gendered horizontal and vertical occupational segregation and the gender pay gap, redistributing responsibility for unpaid care from women to men and state, and prioritising the reconciliation of unpaid care and paid work for both men and women (Orloff, 1993; Fraser, 1998; Lister, 2003; Pascall, 2012).

Equipping women with the ability to exercise agency regarding engagement in unpaid care and paid work is fundamental to this gender-inclusive citizenship framework. For unpaid care to be recognised as a valid citizenship contribution, mothers need to be able to choose to carry out unpaid care (Knijn and Kremer, 1997; Williams, 2001). Similarly, as paid work is also a valid citizenship contribution, mothers should be equally able to choose to engage fully in paid work (Lewis and Giullari, 2005). Enlarging women's agency requires policies that enable women to make genuine choices regarding unpaid care and paid work (see Chapter Two). Affording women the agency to engage in unpaid care and paid work also helps meet the needs of women in their diversity and recognises the life course by enabling women to vary their intensity of engagement in paid work according to their changing circumstances. The next section discusses how Universal Credit can be adapted and implemented to promote a more gender-inclusive concept of citizenship.

Policy recommendations

This study has led to the development of policy recommendations for the Universal Credit conditionality regime that aim to increase the recognition of mothers' caring responsibilities, promote mothers' position in the paid labour market and reduce the current limits placed on their agency. The majority of these recommendations are based on the participants' answers to an interview question regarding how Universal Credit could be improved for them as mothers. Many of the participants expressed the view that personal circumstances, including caring responsibilities, need to be taken into consideration when work-related requirements are set and on an ongoing basis. Suggestions for achieving this include reinstating specialist parent advisors who have an in-depth understanding of caring responsibilities (Wright et al, 2018), allowing more time to develop genuinely tailored Claimant Commitments while ensuring claimants still receive Universal Credit payments (SSAC, 2019) and compiling a standard set of questions that work coaches ask claimants when forming their Claimant Commitments, to ensure appropriate easements are applied (Work and Pensions Committee, 2018a). Additionally, providing work coaches with time to review work-related requirements on an ongoing basis would help to ensure these are appropriate to claimants' changing circumstances (Wright et al, 2018). There is also a need to ensure Claimant Commitments are mutually composed rather than imposed by work coaches. Having a two-stage process for accepting the Claimant Commitment, so that claimants have time to consider whether requirements are appropriate, may help achieve this (Economic Affairs Committee, 2020). Some of the participants also thought that the standard expected number of job search hours should be lowered, as they felt this expectation was unrealistic and lacked recognition of the multitude of activities involved in caring for children and the time and energy this requires.

Another key recommendation arising from the study is the need for a shift in emphasis from sanctions to support (Wright et al, 2018; Economic Affairs Committee, 2020). More meaningful employment-related support is particularly important for addressing the difficulties many mothers experience in entering the paid labour market (see Chapter Five). Reinstating specialist parent advisors would help to achieve this aim, due to their increased understanding of the barriers parents face in obtaining and sustaining paid work (Graham and McQuaid, 2014). Other ways to implement this recommendation include ensuring worksearch review appointments are of a sufficient duration to allow for individualised support (Wright et al, 2018) and incorporating discussions between claimants and their work coaches about long-term career goals and ensuring these are reflected in the Claimant Commitment on an ongoing basis (SSAC, 2019). Additionally, self-employed claimants would benefit from a more flexible approach to reporting earnings (potentially including a longer reporting period) and an increase in the duration of the start-up period (Work and Pensions Committee, 2018c).

The study also highlighted the need for issues with the formal childcare provision within Universal Credit to be addressed, as in many cases these did not facilitate the entrance to and maintenance of paid work (see Chapter Five). The process whereby claimants have to pay for their childcare costs upfront at the beginning of the claim and then claim costs in arrears on an ongoing basis needs to be changed. Options for achieving this include the DWP paying childcare costs to claimants in advance of the care being provided or paying childcare costs directly to childcare providers (Work and Pensions Committee, 2018b). Additionally, communication regarding the formal provision measures should be improved. Mothers need to be informed how much help with childcare costs they are entitled to and, if relevant, given help in calculating these costs when job opportunities arise. A further area for improvement is the JCP environment (see Chapter Four). Several of the participants commented that having a children's area with a selection of toys and books would go a long way to making the JCP environment more child-friendly and supportive. Consideration should also be given to the availability of toilet facilities and accessibility for parents with a child in a pushchair.

As this study shows that main carers of children tend to take responsibility for fulfilling their partners' work-related requirements and demonstrates that they can lose their entire Universal Credit payment if their partner does not comply with mandatory requirements (see Chapter Five), changes need to be made to the joint claim. Liability for fulfilling work-related requirements should be decoupled in joint claims. In some cases, making separate Universal Credit payments to partners in couples may achieve this. However, an alternative solution is needed in cases of couples wherein currently one partner earns a wage from paid employment and the other receives the Universal Credit payment, as in such cases, separating the payment would give the employed partner a larger share of the household income.

More broadly, the study questions the appropriateness of subjecting mothers to conditionality. Problems highlighted in this study that have been documented elsewhere include the inefficacy of sanction-backed conditionality and the adverse impacts caused by the potential for receiving a sanction (Dwyer, 2018a; Wright and Patrick, 2019; Wright et al, 2020). While none of the participants in this study received a sanction, the possibility of this occurring raises considerable ethical questions about the negative impacts on mothers and their children should a sanction be applied (Work and Pensions Committee, 2018a; Wright et al, 2018). Moreover, as previously discussed, this study shows the highly problematic gendered implications of this policy and particularly the issues with making mothers' access to social rights dependent on paid work-related behaviour, as this inherently devalues unpaid care and denies mothers agency. While the policy recommendations can help to mitigate some of these gendered effects, questions remain regarding whether conditionality policies can ever be sufficiently adapted to satisfactorily promote a gender-inclusive concept of citizenship.

The emergence of the COVID-19 pandemic in 2020 has magnified the significance of the gendered impacts of the conditionality within Universal Credit and added urgency to implementing the policy recommendations. Despite record-high levels of employment at the time of the fieldwork, the participants faced difficulties in obtaining, sustaining and progressing in paid work. Therefore, it is highly likely that such difficulties will be exacerbated by the negative impacts the COVID-19 pandemic has had on the paid labour market. Of particular concern, women are more highly concentrated in sectors of the economy which have been particularly affected by the pandemic, such as retail and hospitality (Harding, 2020). Therefore, providing meaningful employment-related support to mothers is imperative. Additionally, it is critical at this juncture that there is consideration of the gendered realities of low-paid work and how these can be addressed so that, going forward, women have a more advantageous position in the UK paid labour market.

The ongoing pandemic and subsequent weaker paid labour market also call into question the ethicality and effectiveness of conditionality and sanctions. While conditionality was suspended during the initial months of the COVID-19 pandemic, it was reintroduced in July 2020. Subjecting claimants to conditionality and sanctions given the current lack of available jobs is unfair and could be counterproductive (Economic Affairs Committee, 2020). The current difficulties claimants are facing in obtaining paid work, which are completely outside their control, further problematise the emphasis within conditionality policies on the supply side, rather than the demand side, in efforts to increase moves from benefits into paid work.

The pandemic has also highlighted women's disproportionate responsibility for unpaid care and has increased this due to the reductions in formal childcare provision (Harding, 2020). At the same time, the necessity of unpaid care has been made more evident. This magnifies problems with the mandatory expectation within Universal Credit for women to undertake extensive work-related requirements and paid work while failing to address, and at times exacerbating, women's disproportionate responsibility for unpaid care. It therefore brings to the fore the need for recognition within Universal Credit policy and practice of what is entailed in caring for children, the difficulties in fully commodifying unpaid care and how unpaid care can make engagement in work-related requirements and paid work difficult. Additionally, there is increased impetus for recognising unpaid care as a valid and essential societal contribution, in part through providing mothers with access to unconditional and sufficient social security payments.

Conclusion

Through tracking mothers' experiences and views over time, the research reported in this book has shown how the conditionality within Universal Credit affects mothers' lives by reducing the quality of care mothers are able to provide, hindering the realisation of long-term career aspirations and limiting choices regarding work–care balance. More broadly, this study adds to the body of literature on conditionality and social citizenship (for example, King, 1999; Paz-Fuchs, 2008; Dwyer, 2016) by examining this relationship from a gender perspective. Crucially, this study shows the ways in which making social rights conditional on paid work-related behaviour and adopting a work first approach while failing to provide adequate employment-related support specifically affects the citizenship status of women. In doing so, it highlights the gendered deficiencies of dominant citizenship frameworks by demonstrating that conceptualising citizenship responsibilities based on masculine patterns of paid work presents difficulties for low-income women who face considerable challenges in engaging in paid work and also devalues unpaid care.

Ultimately, this book has shown that the conditionality regime for main carers of children within Universal Credit constitutes a problematic shift in the social security system that affects the citizenship status of low-income mothers. Analysis of the empirical evidence generated through the study shows that rather than helping to create a citizenship framework that is more inclusive of women, the conditionality furthers an androcentric concept of citizenship and thereby exacerbates women's disadvantaged citizenship status. By making social rights dependent on paid work-related behaviour, conditionality demands women undertake paid work as their active citizenship contribution and increases the devaluation of unpaid care. This is particularly problematic given that unpaid care is an essential and highly important contribution that is disproportionately carried out by women. However, the conditionality within Universal Credit does not recognise or address the gender inequalities mothers face in obtaining paid work, caused in part by their greater responsibility for care. Therefore, the conditionality requires mothers to obtain full citizenship status on the same terms as men without counteracting the significant challenges they face in obtaining and sustaining the types of paid work that would enable them to achieve this. It also places more constraints on mothers in regard to choices around unpaid care and paid work, thereby diminishing women's ability to exercise agency. The combination of these factors results in further excluding low-income mothers, weakening their social positioning and recognition, and eroding a mothering identity which they consider important. It also has negative impacts on their daily lives – for example, in terms of the stress and time poverty incurred.

Given the research findings, this book ultimately calls for social security benefits to be designed and delivered in ways that enhance, rather than undermine, low-income women's citizenship status and do not have negative gendered impacts on their daily lives. This study shows that one crucial means of achieving this is by talking to mothers who are impacted by social security reform. As Jennifer, one of the study's participants, explained with regard to consulting mothers during the policy formation of Universal Credit: "You'd never find something that was perfect for everyone, but to actually consult, I think you would have a different system." Listening to and incorporating the recommendations of mothers when devising and implementing social security reform is one way in which policy makers can ensure recognition is given to a group of women who have been, and are increasingly, designated a lesser citizenship position. Action to create a more gender-inclusive social security system is essential for women in their diversity to obtain full citizenship status in their own right.

References

Abraham, M., Chow, E.N., Maratou-Alipranti, L. and Tastsoglou, E. (2010) 'Rethinking citizenship with women in focus', in M. Abraham, E.N. Chow, L. Maratou-Alipranti and E. Tastsoglou (eds) *Contours of Citizenship*, Farnham: Ashgate, pp 1–22.

Alston, P. (2019) *Visit to the United Kingdom of Great Britain and Northern Ireland: Report of the Special Rapporteur on Extreme Poverty and Human Rights*, New York: United Nations Human Rights Council.

Andersen, K. (2019) 'Universal Credit, gender and unpaid childcare: mothers' accounts of the new welfare conditionality regime', *Critical Social Policy*, 40(3): 430–49.

Annesley, C. (2007) 'Women's political agency and welfare reform: engendering the adult worker model', *Parliamentary Affairs*, 60(3): 452–66.

Annesley, C., Gains, F. and Rummery, K. (2010) 'Engendering politics and policy: the legacy of New Labour', *Policy and Politics*, 38(3): 389–406.

Arni, P., Lalive, R. and van Ours, J.C. (2013) 'How effective are unemployment benefit sanctions? Looking beyond unemployment exit', *Journal of Applied Economics*, 28(7): 1153–78.

Barlow, A., Duncan, S. and James, G. (2002) 'New Labour, the rationality mistake and family policy in Britain', in A.H. Carling, S. Duncan and R. Edwards (eds) *Analysing Families: Morality and Rationality in Policy and Practice*, London: Routledge, pp 110–28.

Bennett, F. (2011) 'White Paper on Universal Credit: written evidence submitted by Fran Bennett', [online] Available from: https://publications.parliament.uk/pa/cm201011/cmselect/cmworpen/743/743we14.htm [Accessed 1 February 2022].

Bennett, F. (2012) 'Universal Credit: overview and gender implications', in M. Kilkey, G. Ramia and K. Farnsworth (eds) *Social Policy Review 24: Analysis and Debate in Social Policy*, Bristol: Policy Press, pp 15–34.

Bennett, F. and Sung, S. (2013a) 'Dimensions of financial autonomy in low-/moderate-income couples from a gender perspective and implications for welfare reform', *Journal of Social Policy*, 42(4): 701–19.

Bennett, F. and Sung, S. (2013b) 'Gender implications of UK welfare reform and government equality duties: evidence from qualitative studies', *Oñati Socio-Legal Series*, 3(7): 1202–21.

Bennett, F. and Sung, S. (2014) 'Money matters: using qualitative research for policy influencing on gender and welfare reform', *Innovation: The European Journal of Social Science Research*, 27(1): 5–19.

Bennett, F. and Daly, M. (2014) Poverty *through a Gender Lens: Evidence and Policy on Gender and Poverty*, Oxford: Department of Social Policy and Intervention, University of Oxford, [online] Available from: www.spi.ox.ac.uk/sites/default/files/Gender_and_poverty_Bennett_and_Daly_final_12_5_14_28_5_14.pdf [Accessed 12 November 2020].

Bergman, S., Hašková, H., Pulkrábková, K., Rantalaiho, M., Valiente, C. and Uhde, Z. (2012) 'Remaking social citizenship in multicultural Europe: women's movements' agency in child-care politics and policies', in B. Halsaa, S. Roseneil and S. Sümer (eds) *Remaking Citizenship in Multicultural Europe: Women's Movements, Gender and Diversity*, Basingstoke: Palgrave Macmillan, pp 94–117.

Beveridge, W. (1942) *Social Insurance and Allied Services*, Cmd 6404, London: HMSO.

Blackburn, S. (1995) 'How useful are feminist theories of the welfare state?', *Women's History Review*, 4(3): 369–94.

Bourdieu, P. (1986) 'The forms of capital', in J.G. Richardson (ed) *Handbook of Theory and Research for the Sociology of Education*, Westport, CT: Greenwood Press, pp 241–58.

Bowlby, S., McKie, L., Gregory, S. and Macpherson, I. (2010) *Interdependency and Care over the Lifecourse*, London: Routledge.

Boyer, K., Dermott, E., James, A. and MacLeavy, J. (2017) 'Men at work? Debating shifting gender divisions of care', *Dialogues in Human Geography*, 7(1): 92–8.

Brewer, M., Finch, D. and Tomlinson, D. (2017) *Universal Remedy: Ensuring Universal Credit is Fit for Purpose*, London: Resolution Foundation.

BSA (British Sociological Association) (2002) 'Statement of ethical practice for the British Sociological Association (March 2002)', [online] Available from: www.britsoc.co.uk/media/23902/statementofethicalpractice.pdf [Accessed 1 February 2022].

Cain, R. (2016) 'Responsibilising recovery: lone and low-paid parents, Universal Credit and the gendered contradictions of UK welfare reform', *British Politics*, 11(4): 488–507.

Cantillon, S. and Lynch, K. (2017) 'Affective equality: love matters', *Hypatia*, 32(1): 169–86.

Caraher, K. and Reuter, E. (2019) 'Mind the gaps: Universal Credit and self-employment in the United Kingdom', *Journal of Poverty and Social Justice*, 27(2): 199–217.

Cass, B. (1994) 'Citizenship, work, and welfare: the dilemma for Australian women', *Social Politics: International Studies in Gender, State and Society*, 1(1): 106–24.

Caswell, D., Kupka, P., Larsen, F. and van Berkel, R. (2017) 'The frontline delivery of welfare-to-work in context' in R. van Berkel, D. Caswell, P. Kupka and F. Larsen (eds) *Frontline Delivery of Welfare-to-Work Policies in Europe: Activating the Unemployed*, London: Routledge, pp 1–11.

Cheetham, M., Moffatt, S., Addison, M. and Wiseman, A. (2019) 'Impact of Universal Credit in North East England: a qualitative study of claimants and support staff', *British Medical Journal Open*, 9(7), Article e029611. dx.doi.org/10.1136/bmjopen-2019-029611

Citizens Advice (2011) 'White Paper on Universal Credit: written evidence submitted by Citizens Advice', [online] Available from: https://publications.parliament.uk/pa/cm201011/cmselect/cmworpen/743/743we56.htm [Accessed 1 February 2022].

City of York Council (2016) 'York economic strategy 2016–2020: an overview of York's economy', [online] Available from: https://democracy.york.gov.uk/documents/s106043/Annex%203%20An%20Overview%20of%20Yorks%20Economy.pdf [Accessed 19 August 2020].

Coleman, N. and Riley, T. (2012) *Lone Parent Obligations: Following Lone Parents' Journeys from Benefits to Work*, London: DWP.

Cominetti, N., Henehan, K. and Clarke, S. (2019) *Low Pay Britain 2019*, London: Resolution Foundation.

Conaghan, J. (2009) *Gendered Aspects of Activation Policies: The Limits of Welfare to Work*, Oxford: Foundation of Law, Justice and Society, [online] Available from: www.fljs.org/content/gendered-aspects-activation-policies-limits-welfare-work [Accessed 1 February 2022].

Corden, A. and Millar, J. (2007) 'Qualitative longitudinal research for social policy—introduction to themed section', *Social Policy and Society*, 6(4): 529–32.

Corden, A. and Nice, K. (2007) 'Qualitative longitudinal analysis for policy: incapacity benefits recipients taking part in Pathways to Work', *Social Policy and Society*, 6(4): 557–69.

Costa Dias, M., Joyce, R. and Parodi, F. (2018) 'Mothers suffer big long-term pay penalty from part-time working', *IFS*, [online] Available from: www.ifs.org.uk/publications/10364 [Accessed 11 June 2020].

Couling, N. (2016) 'Digital welfare (II): transformation through technology', *Reform*, [online] Available from: www.reform.uk/reformer/digital-welfare-ii-transformation-through-technology/ [Accessed 7 November 2017].

CPAG (Child Action Poverty Group) (2015a) *The Welfare Reform and Work Bill: Does It Comply with Human Rights? Response to the Call for Evidence from the Joint Committee on Human Rights*, London: CPAG.

CPAG (2015b) *Welfare Reform and Work Bill. Commons Second Reading Briefing: 20 July 2015*, London: CPAG.

Crisp, R., Batty, E. and Cole, I. (2009) *Work and Worklessness in Deprived Neighbourhoods*, York: Joseph Rowntree Foundation.

Daly, M. (2011) 'What adult worker model? A critical look at recent social policy reform in Europe from a gender and family perspective', *Social Politics*, 18(1): 1–23.

D'Arcy, C. and Finch, D. (2017) *The Great Escape? Low Pay and Progression in the UK's Labour Market*, London: Social Mobility Commission.

Davies, L. (2012) 'Single parents: unemployed or otherwise engaged?', *People, Place and Policy Online*, 6(1): 16–28.

Davies, L. (2015) 'Nudged into employment: single parents and welfare reform', in M. Harrison and T. Sanders (eds) *Social Policies and Social Control: New Perspectives*, Bristol: Policy Press, pp 151–66.

Deacon, A. (2004) 'Justifying conditionality: the case of anti-social tenants', *Housing Studies*, 19(6): 911–26.

Deacon, A. and Patrick, R. (2011) 'A new welfare settlement? The Coalition government and welfare-to-work', in H.M. Bochel (ed) *The Conservative Party and Social Policy*, Bristol: Policy Press, pp 161–79.

Dean, H. (2001) 'Welfare rights and the "workfare state"', *Benefits*, 30: 1–4.

De Henau, J. (2018) Social Security and Women: Briefing from the UK Women's Budget Group on the Impact of Cuts to Social Security Benefits since 2010 on Women, Women's Budget Group, [online] Available at: https://wbg.org.uk/wp-content/uploads/2018/10/Social-Security-November-2018-w-cover.pdf [Accessed 7 October 2020].

De Henau, J., Harris, S. and Stephenson, M-A. (2018) *Women, Employment and Earnings*, London: Women's Budget Group.

Dewar, L. and Ben-Galim, D. (2017) *An Impossible Bind: Requirements to Work under Universal Credit*, London: Gingerbread.

Dorsett, R., Haile, G. and Speckesser, S. (2006) *Work Focused Interviews for Partners and Enhanced New Deal for Partners: Quantitative Impact Assessment*, Department for Work and Pensions Research Report No 352, Leeds: Corporate Document Services.

Duncan, S. and Edwards, R. (1999) *Single Mothers, Paid Work and Gendered Moral Rationalities*, Basingstoke: Palgrave Macmillan.

Duncan, S. and Smith, D. (2002) 'Geographies of family formations: spatial differences and gender cultures in Britain', *Transactions of the Institute of British Geographers*, 27(4): 471–93.

Duncan, S., Edwards, R., Reynolds, T. and Alldred, P. (2003) 'Motherhood, paid work and partnering: values and theories', *Work, Employment and Society*, 17(2): 309–30.

Duncan Smith, I. (2010) 'Universal Credit: welfare that works', Speech by the Rt Hon Iain Duncan Smith MP, Secretary of State for Work and Pensions, 11 November, [online] Available from: www.gov.uk/government/speeches/universal-credit-welfare-that-works [Accessed 9 October 2020].

Duncan Smith, I. (2017) 'The CSJ story', *Centre for Social Justice*, [online] Available from: www.centreforsocialjustice.org.uk/about/story [Accessed 11 November 2017].

Durbin, S., Page, M. and Walby, S. (2017) 'Gender equality and "austerity": vulnerabilities, resistance and change', *Gender, Work, and Organization*, 24(1): 1–6.

DWP (Department for Work and Pensions) (2008) *Raising Expectations and Increasing Support: Reforming Welfare for the Future*, London: DWP.

DWP (2010a) *21st Century Welfare*, London: DWP.

DWP (2010b) *Equality Impact Assessment. Universal Credit: Welfare that Works*, London: DWP.

DWP (2010c) *Universal Credit: Welfare that Works*, London: DWP.

DWP (2011a) *Conditionality, Sanctions and Hardship: Equality Impact Assessment*, London: DWP.

DWP (2011b) *Impact Assessment: Conditionality Measures in the 2011 Welfare Reform Bill*, London: DWP.

DWP (2012a) *DWP's Digital Strategy*, London: DWP.

DWP (2012b) *Universal Credit Evaluation Framework*, London: DWP.

DWP (2012c) *Universal Credit: Impact Assessment*, London: DWP.

DWP (2014a) *Universal Credit at Work*, London: DWP.

DWP (2014b) *Universal Credit: Increasing the Childcare Offer*, London: DWP.

DWP (2015a) *Universal Credit at Work: Spring 2015*, London: DWP.

DW (2015b) *Universal Credit at Work: December 2015*, London: DWP.

DWP (2015c) *Welfare Reform and Work Bill: Impact Assessment of the Change in Conditionality for Responsible Carers on Universal Credit*, London: DWP.

DWP (2016) *Universal Credit Evaluation Framework 2016*, London: DWP.

DWP (2017a) 'Advice for decision making: staff guide. Chapter J2: work-related groups', [online] Available from: https://assets.publishing.service.gov.uk/government/uploads/system/uploads/attachment_data/file/661700/admj2.pdf [Accessed 7 February 2022].

DWP (2017b) *Understanding How Universal Credit Affects Employment Behaviour*, London: DWP.

DWP (2018a) 'Advice for decision making: staff guide. Chapter J3: work-related requirements', [online] Available from: https://assets.publishing.service.gov.uk/government/uploads/system/uploads/attachment_data/file/702975/admj3.pdf [Accessed 7 February 2022].

DWP (2018b) 'Written evidence from the Department of Work and Pensions (ANC0083)', [online] Available from: http://data.parliament.uk/writtenevidence/committeeevidence.svc/evidencedocument/work-and-pensions-committee/benefit-sanctions/written/84015.pdf [Accessed 8 January 2021].

DWP (2019a) 'A7/2018 (revised) Universal Credit full service areas: Guidance for local authorities', [online] Available from: www.gov.uk/government/publications/housing-benefit-adjudication-circulars-2018/a72018-universal-credit-full-service-areas-guidance-for-local-authorities [Accessed 10 November 2020].

DWP (2019b) *Households below Average Income: An Analysis of the UK Income Distribution: 1994/95–2017/18*, London: DWP.

DWP (2020a) 'Universal Credit and you', [online] Available from: www.gov.uk/government/publications/universal-credit-and-you/universal-credit-and-you-a [Accessed 15 January 2020].

DWP (2020b) 'Universal Credit and your Claimant Commitment', [online] Available from: https://www.gov.uk/government/publications/universal-credit-and-your-claimant-commitment-quick-guide/universal-credit-and-your-claimant-commitment [Accessed 12 March 2020].

DWP (2020c) 'Universal Credit: childcare guide', [online] Available from: www.gov.uk/government/publications/universal-credit-and-childcare/universal-credit-childcare-guide [Accessed 28 February 2020].

DWP (2020d) 'Universal Credit for the self-employed', [online] Available from: www.gov.uk/government/publications/universal-credit-and-self-employment-quick-guide/universal-credit-and-self-employment-quick-guide [Accessed 6 March 2020].

DWP (2020e) 'Universal Credit: further information for families', [online] Available from: www.gov.uk/government/publications/universal-credit-and-your-family-quick-guide/universal-credit-further-information-for-families [Accessed 18 April 2018].

Dwyer, P. (1998) 'Conditional citizens? Welfare rights and responsibilities in the late 1990s', *Critical Social Policy*, 18(57): 493–517.

Dwyer, P. (2000) *Welfare Rights and Responsibilities: Contesting Social Citizenship*, Bristol: Policy Press.

Dwyer, P. (2004) 'Creeping conditionality in the UK: from welfare rights to conditional entitlements?', *Canadian Journal of Sociology*, 29(2): 265–87.

Dwyer, P. (2010) *Understanding Social Citizenship: Themes and Perspectives for Policy and Practice* (2nd edn), Bristol: Policy Press.

Dwyer, P. (2016) 'Citizenship, conduct and conditionality: sanction and support in the 21st-century UK welfare state', in Z. Irving, M. Fenger and J. Hudson (eds) *Social Policy Review 28: Analysis and Debate in Social Policy*, Bristol: Policy Press, pp 41–61.

Dwyer, P. (2018a) Final Findings Report: Welfare Conditionality Project 2013–2018, York: Welfare Conditionality Project, [online] Available from: www.welfareconditionality.ac.uk/wp-content/uploads/2018/06/40475_Welfare-Conditionality_Report_complete-v3.pdf [Accessed 7 March 2020]

Dwyer, P. (2018b) 'Punitive and ineffective: benefit sanctions within social security', *Journal of Social Security Law*, 25(3): 142–57.

Dwyer, P. and Ellison, N. (2009a) '"We nicked stuff from all over the place": policy transfer or muddling through?' *Policy and Politics*, 37(3): 389–407.

Dwyer, P. and Ellison, N. (2009b) 'Work and welfare: the rights and responsibilities of unemployment in the UK', in M. Giugni (ed) *The Politics of Unemployment in Europe: Policy Responses and Collective Action*, London: Routledge, pp 53–66.

Dwyer, P. and Wright, S. (2014) 'Universal Credit, ubiquitous conditionality and its implications for social citizenship', *Journal of Poverty and Social Justice*, 22(1): 27–35.

Economic Affairs Committee (2020) *Universal Credit Isn't Working: Proposals for Reform*, London: House of Lords.

Edmiston, D. (2018) *Welfare, Inequality and Social Citizenship: Deprivation and Affluence in Austerity Britain*, Bristol: Policy Press.

Elliott, J. (2005) *Using Narrative in Social Research: Qualitative and Quantitative Approaches*, London: Sage.

Etherington, D. and Daguerre, A. (2015) *Welfare Reform Work First Policies and Benefit Conditionality: Reinforcing Poverty and Social Exclusion?* London: Centre for Enterprise and Economic Development Research.

Falkingham, J., Evandrou, M. and Vlachantoni, A. (2014) *Exploring the Link between Demographic Change and Poverty in the UK*, Southampton: ESRC Centre for Population Change.

Fawcett Society (2015) *Where's the Benefit? An Independent Inquiry into Women and Jobseeker's Allowance*, London: Fawcett Society.

Field, F. and Forsey, A. (2016) *Fixing Broken Britain? An Audit of Working-age Welfare Reform since 2010*, London: Civitas.

Finch, D. (2015) *Making the Most of UC: Final Report of the Resolution Foundation Review of Universal Credit*, London: Resolution Foundation.

Finch, D. (2016) *Universal Challenge: Making a Success of Universal Credit*, London: Resolution Foundation.

Finn, P. (2018) *Playing with the Absurdity of Welfare: Experiences of Irish Welfare Conditionality*, Unpublished PhD, Maynooth University.

Finn, P. (2020) *Navigating the absurdity of Irish welfare, Welfare Conditionality*, 6 February, [online] Available from: www.welfareconditionality.ac.uk/2020/02/navigating-the-absurdity-of-irish-welfare/ [Accessed 23 March 2020].

Fletcher, D.R. (2011) 'Welfare reform, Jobcentre Plus and the street-level bureaucracy: towards inconsistent and discriminatory welfare for severely disadvantaged groups?', *Social Policy and Society*, 10(4): 445–58.

Fletcher, D.R. and Wright, S. (2018) 'A hand up or a slap down? Criminalising benefit claimants in Britain via strategies of surveillance, sanctions and deterrence', *Critical Social Policy*, 38(2): 323–44.

Fraser, N. (1994) 'After the family wage: gender equity and the welfare state', *Political Theory*, 22(4): 591–618.

Fraser, N. (1998) 'Social justice in the age of identity politics: redistribution, recognition and participation', in G.B. Peterson (ed) *Tanner Lectures on Human Values, Vol 19*, Salt Lake City, UT: The University of Utah Press, pp 1–67.

Fraser, N. and Gordon, L. (1994) '"Dependency" demystified: inscriptions of power in a keyword of the welfare state', *Social Politics*, 1(1): 4–31.

Freedland, M. and King, D. (2003) 'Contractual governance and illiberal contracts: some problems of contractualism as an instrument of behaviour management by agencies of government', *Cambridge Journal of Economics*, 27(3): 465–77.

Friedli, L. and Stearn, R. (2015) 'Positive affect as coercive strategy: conditionality, activation and the role of psychology in UK government workfare programmes', *Medical Humanities*, 41(1): 40–7.

Gillies, V. (2007) *Marginalised Mothers: Exploring Working-class Experiences of Parenting*, Abingdon: Routledge.

Gingerbread (2013) *Job Seeking Requirements for Single Parents under Universal Credit: Briefing Note for Parliamentarians on the Universal Credit Regulations 2013*, London: Gingerbread.

Gingerbread (2015) 'Welfare Reform and Work Bill 2015–16. Gingerbread briefing: House of Commons committee stage', [online] Available from: www.cpag.org.uk/sites/default/files/uploads/Gingerbread%20151013%20Welfare%20Reform%20and%20Work%20Bill%20-%20HoC%20committee%20stage%20submission_0.pdf [Accessed 2 February 2022].

Goodin, R.E. (2001) 'False principles of welfare reform', *The Australian Journal of Social Issues*, 36(3): 189–205.

Goodin, R.E. (2002) 'Structures of mutual obligation', *Journal of Social Policy*, 31(4): 579–96.

Goodwin, V. (2008) *The Effects of Sanctions on Single Parents' Employment Decisions and Moves into Employment*, Research Report No 511, London: DWP.

Gould, C.C. (1983) 'Private rights and public virtues: women, the family and democracy', in C.C. Gould (ed) *Beyond Domination: New Perspectives on Women and Philosophy*, Totwa: Rowman and Allanheld, pp 3–18.

Grabham, E. and Smith, J. (2010) 'From social security to individual responsibility (part two): writing off poor women's work in the Welfare Reform Act 2009', *The Journal of Social Welfare and Family Law*, 32(1): 81–93.

Graham, H. and McQuaid, R. (2014) Exploring the Impacts of the UK Government's Welfare Reforms on Single Parents Moving into Work, [online] Available from: https://dspace.stir.ac.uk/bitstream/1893/20443/1/Lone_parents_Full_Report_FINAL%200514.pdf [Accessed 12 November 2020].

Grant, L. (2009) 'Women's disconnection from local labour markets: real lives and policy failure', *Critical Social Policy*, 29(3): 330–50.

Gray, C. (2017) *A Crying Shame: Affect, Emotion and Welfare Receipt in New Zealand*, Unpublished PhD, University of Canterbury.

Griffiths, R., Wood, M., Bennett, F. and Millar, J. (2020) *Uncharted Territory: Universal Credit, Couples and Money*, Bath: Institute for Policy Research.

Griggs, J. and Evans, M. (2010) *Sanctions within Conditional Benefit Systems: A Review of Evidence*, York: Joseph Rowntree Foundation.

Griggs, J., Hammond, A. and Walker, R. (2014) 'Activations for all', in I. Lodemel and A. Moreria (eds) *Activation or Workfare? Governance and the Neo-liberal Convergence*, Oxford: Oxford University Press, pp 73–100.

Grover, C. (2007) 'The Freud Report on the future of welfare to work: some critical reflections', *Critical Social Policy*, 27(4): 534–45.

Grover, C. (2012) '"Personalised conditionality": observations on active proletarianisation in late modern Britain', *Capital and Class*, 36(2): 283–301.

Haddon, C. (2012) *Making Policy in Opposition: The Development of Universal Credit, 2005–2010*, London: Institute for Government.

Hancock, L. (2000) 'Gendered citizenship in Britain: from mother-care to worker', in A. Vandenberg (ed) *Citizenship and Democracy in a Global Era*, Basingstoke: Macmillan Press, pp 156–70.

Harding, S. (2020) *The Impact of Universal Credit on Women*, Belfast: Women's Regional Consortium.

Harrison, M. and Sanders, T. (2014) 'Introduction', in M. Harrison and T. Sanders (eds) *Social Policies and Social Control: New Perspectives on the 'Not-so-Big Society'*, Bristol: Policy Press, pp 3–22.

Haux, T. (2012) 'Activating single parents: an evidence-based policy appraisal of welfare-to-work reform in Britain', *Social Policy and Society*, 11(1): 1–14.

Haux, T., Salmon, D., Taylor, L., Deave, T., Cohen, S., Dewar, L. and Samelius, T. (2012) *A Longitudinal Qualitative Study of the Journeys of Single Parents on Jobseeker's Allowance*, Bristol: Single Parent Action Network and University of the West of England.

Haylett, C. (2003) Class, care, and welfare reform: reading meanings, talking feelings, *Environment and Planning A*, 35(5): 799–814.

HMG (Her Majesty's Government) (2018) 'Help paying for childcare', [online] Available from: www.gov.uk/help-with-childcare-costs/free-childcare-and-education-for-2-to-4-year-olds [Accessed 8 February 2022].

HMG (2020) 'How to claim Universal Credit: step by step', [online] Available from: https://www.gov.uk/how-to-claim-universal-credit [Accessed 6 March 2020].

Hobson, B. (1990) 'No exit, no voice: women's economic dependency and the welfare state', *Acta Sociologica*, 33(3): 235–50.

Holloway, S.L. and Pimlott-Wilson, H. (2016) 'New economy, neoliberal state and professionalised parenting: mothers' labour market engagement and state support for social reproduction in class-differentiated Britain', *Transactions of the Institute of British Geographers*, 41(4): 376–88.

House of Commons Library (2021) 'Constituency data: Universal Credit rollout', [online] Available from: https://commonslibrary.parliament.uk/social-policy/welfare-pensions/benefits/constituency-data-universal-credit-roll-out/ [Accessed 22 December 2021].

House of Lords Hansard (2015a) 'Welfare Reform and Work Bill, 9 December 2015', col 1653, [online] Available from: https://publications.parliament.uk/pa/ld201516/ldhansrd/text/151209-0003.htm [Accessed 22 December 2021].

House of Lords Hansard (2015b) 'Welfare Reform and Work Bill, 9 December 2015', col 1658, Available at: https://publications.parliament.uk/pa/ld201516/ldhansrd/text/151209-0003.htm [Accessed 22 December 2021].

Ingold, J. and Etherington, D. (2013) 'Work, welfare and gender inequalities: an analysis of activation strategies for partnered women in the UK, Australia and Denmark', *Work, Employment and Society*, 27(4): 621–38.

Innes, S. and Scott, G. (2003) '"After I've done the mum things": women, care and transitions', *Sociological Research Online*, 8(4): 39–52.

Javornik, J. and Ingold, J. (2015) 'A childcare system fit for the future?', in L. Foster, A. Brunton, C. Deeming and T. Haux (eds) *In Defense of Welfare II*, Bristol: Policy Press, pp 75–8.

Jensen, P.H. and Møberg, R.J. (2017) 'Does women's employment enhance women's citizenship?', *European Societies*, 19(2): 178–201.

Johnsen, S. (2014) Conditionality Briefing: Single Parents, [online] Available from: www.welfareconditionality.ac.uk/wp-content/uploads/2014/09/Briefing_LoneParents_14.09.10_FINAL.pdf [Accessed 13 November 2020].

Johnsen, S. (2016) First Wave Findings: Single Parents, [online] Available from: www.welfareconditionality.ac.uk/wp-content/uploads/2016/05/WelCond-findings-lone-parents-May16.pdf [Accessed 15 January 2018].

Johnsen, S. and Blenkinsopp, J. (2018) 'Final Findings: Single Parents', [online] Available from: www.welfareconditionality.ac.uk/wp-content/uploads/2018/05/39273-Lone-parents-web.pdf [Accessed 4 June 2018].

Judge, L. (2013) *Will Universal Credit Work?*, London: Child Poverty Action Group.

Judge, L. (2015) *Round the Clock: In-work Poverty and the 'Hours Question'*, London: Child Poverty Action Group.

Jun, M. (2015) *Single Mothers in the UK, Have Their Lives Got Better since the Transition from Welfare to Work?* Unpublished PhD, University of York.

Jun, M. (2019) 'Stigma and shame attached to claiming social assistance benefits: understanding the detrimental impact on UK single mothers' social relationships', *Journal of Family Studies*, Advance online publication: doi.org/10.1080/13229400.2019.1689840.

Jupp, E., Bowlby, S., Franklin, J. and Hall, S.M. (2019) *The New Politics of Home: Housing, Gender and Care in Times of Crisis*, Bristol: Policy Press.

Kennedy, S. (2010) *Single Parents and Jobseeker's Allowance*, London: House of Commons Library.

Kennedy, S. and Keen, R. (2016) *Briefing Paper: Benefit Claimants Sanctions (Required Assessment) Bill 2016–17*, London: House of Commons Library.

Kennedy, S. and Keen, R. (2018) *Universal Credit Roll-out: 2018–19*, London: House of Commons Library.

Kennedy, S., Keen, R. and Wilson, W. (2017) *Debate Pack: Impact of DWP Policies on Low Income Households*, London: House of Commons Library.

King, D. (1999) *In the Name of Liberalism: Illiberal Social Policy in the USA and Britain*, Oxford: Oxford University Press.

Kingfisher, C. (2002) 'Part I. The big picture: globalization, neoliberalism, and the feminization of poverty', in C. Kingfisher (ed) *Western Welfare in Decline: Globalization and Women's Poverty*, Philadelphia: University of Pennsylvania Press, pp 3–61.

Knijn, T. and Kremer, M. (1997) 'Gender and the caring dimension of welfare states: toward inclusive citizenship', *Social Politics*, 4(3): 328–61.

Kowalewska, H. (2015) 'Diminishing returns: single mothers' financial work incentives and incomes under the coalition', *Social Policy and Society*, 14(4): 569–91.

Letablier, M-T., Eydoux, A. and Betzelt, S. (2011) 'Social citizenship and activation in Europe: a gendered perspective', in S. Betzelt and S. Bothfeld (eds) *Activation and Labour Market Reforms in Europe*, Basingstoke: Palgrave Macmillan, pp 79–100.

Lewis, J. (1997) 'Gender and welfare regimes: further thoughts', *Social Politics*, 4(2): 160–77.

Lewis, J. (2002) 'Individualisation, assumptions about the existence of an adult worker model and the shift towards contractualism', in A.H. Carling, S. Duncan and R. Edwards (eds) *Analysing Families: Morality and Rationality in Policy and Practice*, London: Routledge, pp 51–6.

Lewis, J. (2007) 'Analysing qualitative longitudinal research in evaluations', *Social Policy and Society*, 6(4): 545–56.

Lewis, J. (2009) *Work-family Balance, Gender and Policy*, Cheltenham: Edward Elgar.

Lewis, J. and Giullari, S. (2005) 'The adult worker model family, gender equality and care: the search for new policy principles and the possibilities and problems of a capabilities approach', *Economy and Society*, 34(1): 76–104.

Lindsay, C., McQuaid, R. and Dutton, M. (2007) 'New approaches to employability in the UK: combining "human capital development" and "work first" strategies?', *Journal of Social Policy*, 36(4): 539–60.

Lipsky, M. (2010) *Street-level Bureaucracy: Dilemmas of the Individual in Public Services*, New York: Russell Sage Foundation.

Lister, R. (2000a) 'Dilemmas in engendering citizenship', in B. Hobson (ed) *Gender and Citizenship in Transition*, Basingstoke: Macmillan Press, pp 33–83.

Lister, R. (2000b) 'Gender and the analysis of social policy', in G. Lewis, S. Gerwitz and J. Clarke (eds) *Rethinking Social Policy*, London: Sage, pp 22–35.

Lister, R. (2001) 'Towards a citizens' welfare state', *Theory, Culture & Society*, 18(2–3): 91–111.

Lister, R. (2003) *Citizenship: Feminist Perspectives* (2nd edn), Basingstoke: Palgrave Macmillan.

Lister, R. (2004) *Poverty: Key Concepts*, Cambridge: Polity Press.

Lister, R. (2007) 'Inclusive citizenship: realizing the potential', *Citizenship Studies*, 11(1): 49–61.

Lister, R. (2011) 'The age of responsibility: social policy and citizenship in the early 21st century', in C. Holden, M. Kilkey and G. Ramia (eds) *Social Policy Review 23: Analysis and Debate in Social Policy*, Bristol: Policy Press, pp 63–84.

Loopstra, R., Reeves, A., McKee, M. and Stuckler, D. (2015) Do Punitive Approaches to Unemployment Benefit Recipients Increase Welfare Exit and Employment? A Cross-area Analysis of UK Sanctioning Reforms, Sociology Working Papers, [online] Available at: http://aaronreeves.org/Loopstra_sanction120115-2_WorkingPaperCopy.pdf [Accessed 23 February 2022].

Lynch, K. and Lyons, M. (2009) 'Care-less citizenship? Public devaluation and private validation', in K. Lynch, J. Baker and M. Lyons (eds) *Affective Equality: Love, Care and Injustice*, Basingstoke: Palgrave Macmillan, pp 78–92.

Lynch, K. and Walsh, J. (2009) 'Love, care and solidarity: what is and is not commodifiable', in K. Lynch, J. Baker and M. Lyons (eds) *Affective Equality: Love, Care and Injustice*, Basingstoke: Palgrave Macmillan, pp 35–53.

Macdonald, R., Shildrick, T. and Furlong, A. (2014) 'In search of "intergenerational cultures of worklessness": hunting the Yeti and shooting zombies', *Critical Social Policy*, 34(2): 199–220.

MacLeavy, J. (2007) 'Engendering New Labour's workfarist regime: exploring the intersection of welfare state restructuring and labour market policies in the UK', *Gender, Place and Culture*, 14(6): 721–43.

MacLeavy, J. (2011) 'A "new politics" of austerity, workfare and gender? The UK coalition government's welfare reform proposals', *Cambridge Journal of Regions, Economy and Society*, 4(3): 355–67.

Marshall, T.H. (1950) *Citizenship and Social Class*, Cambridge: Cambridge University Press.

McDonough, K. (2019) *It's Just Constant Debt: Why Parents Need Better Support for Childcare under Universal Credit*, London: Save the Children.

McDowell, L. (2005) 'Love, money, and gender divisions of labour: some critical reflections on welfare-to-work policies in the UK', *Journal of Economic Geography*, 5(3): 365–79.

McDowell, L. and Dyson, J. (2011) 'The other side of the knowledge economy: "reproductive" employment and affective labours in Oxford', *Environment and Planning A*, 43(9): 2186–201.

McKechnie, K. (2019) 'Early warning system report on Universal Credit and childcare costs', *CPAG*, [online] Available from: https://cpag.org.uk/policy-and-campaigns/report/early-warning-system-report-universal-credit-and-childcare-costs [Accessed 22 February 2020].

McNay, L. (2016) 'Agency', in L. Disch and M. Hawkesworth (eds) *The Oxford Handbook of Feminist Theory*, New York: Oxford University Press, pp 39–60.

Millar, J. (2015) 'Policy briefing: Universal Credit – is it worth it?', *Discover Society*, [online] Available from: https://discoversociety.org/2015/01/03/policy-briefing-universal-credit-is-it-worth-it/ [Accessed 13 November 2020].

Millar, J. (2019) 'Self-responsibility and activation for single mothers in the United Kingdom', *The American Behavioral Scientist*, 63(1): 85–99.

Millar, J. and Bennett, F. (2017) 'Universal Credit: assumptions, contradictions and virtual reality', *Social Policy and Society*, 16(2): 169–82.

Millar, J. and Ridge, T. (2009) 'Relationships of care: working single mothers, their children and employment sustainability', *Journal of Social Policy*, 38(1): 103–21.

Millar, J. and Ridge, T. (2020) 'No margin for error: fifteen years in the working lives of single mothers and their children', *Journal of Social Policy*, 49(1): 1–17.

Miller, T. (2015) 'Going back: "stalking", talking and researcher responsibilities in qualitative longitudinal research', *International Journal of Social Research Methodology*, 18(3): 293–305.

National Audit Office (2016) *Benefit Sanctions*, HC 628. London: National Audit Office.

National Audit Office (2018) *Rolling Out Universal Credit*, HC 1123, London: National Audit Office.

Neale, B. (2012) Qualitative Longitudinal Research: An Introduction to the Timescapes Methods Guide Series, Timescapes Method Guides Series, Leeds: Timescapes.

Neale, B. (2015) 'Time and the lifecourse: perspectives from qualitative longitudinal research', in N. Worth and I. Hardill (eds) *Researching the Lifecourse: Critical Reflections from the Social Sciences*, Bristol: Policy Press, pp 25–41.

Neale, B. and Flowerdew, J. (2003) 'Time, texture and childhood: the contours of longitudinal qualitative research', *International Journal of Social Research Methodology*, 6(3): 189–99.

Neitzert, E. (2020) Spirals of Inequality: How Unpaid Care Is at the Heart of Gender Inequalities, Commission on a Gender-equal Economy and Women's Budget Group, [online] Available from: https://wbg.org.uk/wp-content/uploads/2020/04/Accompanying-paper-FINAL.pdf [Accessed 11 June 2020].

Nightingale, M. (2020) 'Stepping-stone or dead end: to what extent does part-time employment enable progression out of low pay for male and female employees in the UK?' *Journal of Social Policy*, 49(1): 41–59.

Nothdurfter, U. (2016) 'The street-level delivery of activation policies: constraints and possibilities for a practice of citizenship', *European Journal of Social Work*, 19(3–4): 420–40.

Nussbaum, M. (2003) 'Capabilities as fundamental entitlements: Sen and social justice', *Feminist Economics*, 9(2–3): 33–59.

O'Connor, J.S. (2006) 'Gender, citizenship and welfare state regimes', in P. Kennett (ed) *A Handbook of Comparative Social Policy*, Cheltenham: Edward Elgar, pp 180–200.

ONS (Office for National Statistics) (2018) 'Household satellite account, UK: 2015 and 2016', [online] Available at: www.ons.gov.uk/economy/nationalaccounts/satelliteaccounts/articles/householdsatelliteaccounts/2015and2016estimates [Accessed 5 June 2020].

ONS (2019a) 'Births in England and Wales: 2018', [online] Available from: www.ons.gov.uk/peoplepopulationandcommunity/birthsdeathsandmarriages/livebirths/bulletins/birthsummarytablesenglandandwales/2018 [Accessed 11 June 2020].

ONS (2019b) 'Disability and employment, UK: 2019', [online] Available from: www.ons.gov.uk/peoplepopulationandcommunity/healthandsocialcare/disability/bulletins/disabilityandemploymentuk/2019 [Accessed 11 June 2020].

ONS (2019c) 'Labour market profile – York', [online] Available from: www.nomisweb.co.uk/reports/lmp/la/1946157112/report.aspx#tabempunemp [Accessed 25 July 2019].

ONS (2020) 'Marriages in England and Wales: 2017', [online] Available from: www.ons.gov.uk/peoplepopulationandcommunity/birthsdeathsandmarriages/marriagecohabitationandcivilpartnerships/bulletins/marriagesinenglandandwalesprovisional/2017 [Accessed 10 August 2020].

Orloff, A.S. (1993) 'Gender and the social rights of citizenship: the comparative analysis of gender relations and welfare states', *American Sociological Review*, 58(3): 303–28.

Orloff, A.S. (2006) 'From maternalism to "employment for all": state policies to promote women's employment across the affluent democracies', in J.D. Levy (ed) *The State after Statism: New State Activities in the Age of Liberalization*, Harvard: Harvard University Press, pp 230–70.

Orloff, A.S. (2009) 'Gendering the comparative analysis of welfare states: an unfinished agenda', *Sociological Theory*, 27(3): 317–43.

Pascall, G. (1997) *Social Policy: A New Feminist Analysis*, London: Routledge.

Pascall, G. (2012) *Gender Equality in the Welfare State?*, Bristol: Policy Press.

Pateman, C. (1989) *The Disorder of Women*, Cambridge: Polity Press.

Pateman, C. (2005) 'Another way forward: welfare, social reproduction, and a basic income', in L.M. Mead and C. Beem (eds) *Welfare Reform and Political Theory*, New York: Russell Sage Foundation, pp 34–64.

Patrick, R. (2011) 'Disabling or enabling: the extension of work-related conditionality to disabled people', *Social Policy and Society*, 10(3): 309–20.

Patrick, R. (2012) 'Work as the primary "duty" of the responsible citizen: a critique of this work-centric approach', *People, Place and Policy Online*, 6(1): 5–15.

Patrick, R. (2014) 'Working on welfare: findings from a qualitative longitudinal study into the lived experiences of welfare reform in the UK', *Journal of Social Policy*, 43(4): 705–25.

Patrick, R. (2017) *For whose Benefit? The Everyday Realities of Welfare Reform*, Bristol: Policy Press.

Patrick, R. and Simpson, M. (2020) *Universal Credit Could Be a Lifeline in Northern Ireland, but It Must Be Designed with People Who Use It*, York: Joseph Rowntree Foundation.

Paz-Fuchs, A. (2008) *Welfare to Work: Conditional Rights in Social Policy*, Oxford: Oxford University Press.

Pearce, D., 1990. 'Welfare is not for women: Why the war on poverty cannot conquer the feminization of poverty' in: L. Gordon (ed) *Women, the State, and Welfare*, London: University of Wisconsin Press, pp 265–79.

Petrongolo, B. (2009) 'The long-term effects of job search requirements: evidence from the UK JSA reform', *Journal of Public Economics*, 93(11): 1234–53.

Pulkingham, J., Fuller, S. and Kershaw, P. (2010) 'Single motherhood, welfare reform and active citizen subjectivity', *Critical Social Policy*, 30(2): 267–91.

Rafferty, A. (2014) 'Gender equality and the impact of recession and austerity in the UK', *Revue de l'OFCE*, 2(133): 335–61.

Rafferty, A. and Wiggan, J. (2017) 'The time-related underemployment of lone parents during welfare reform, recession and austerity: a challenge to in-work conditionality?' *Social Policy and Administration*, 51(3): 511–38.

Reeves, A. (2017) 'Does sanctioning disabled claimants of unemployment insurance increase labour market inactivity? An analysis of 346 British local authorities between 2009 and 2014', *Journal of Poverty and Social Justice*, 25(2): 129–46.

Reeves, A. and Loopstra, R. (2017) '"Set up to fail"? How welfare conditionality undermines citizenship for vulnerable groups', *Social Policy and Society*, 16(2): 327–38.

Reis, S. (2018) *The Female Face of Poverty: Examining the Cause and Consequences of Economic Deprivation for Women*, London: Women's Budget Group.

Ribbens McCarthy, J. and Edwards, R. (2002) 'The individual in public and private: the significance of mothers and children', in A. Carling, S. Duncan and R. Edwards (eds) *Analysing Families: Morality and Rationality in Policy and Practice*, London: Routledge, pp 199–217.

Richards-Gray, L. (2020) 'Political discourse and gendered welfare reform: a case study of the UK Coalition government', *Journal of Elections, Public Opinion and Parties*, Advance online publication. doi.org/10.1080/17457289.2020.1760283

Roantree, B. and Vira, K. (2018) *The Rise and Rise of Women's Employment in the UK*, London: Institute for Fiscal Studies.

Robertson, L., Wright, S. and Stewart, A.B.R. (2020) *How Well Is Universal Credit Supporting People in Glasgow?*, York: Joseph Rowntree Foundation.

Roseneil, S., Halsaa, B. and Sümer, S. (2012) 'Remaking citizenship in multicultural Europe: women's movements, gender and diversity', in B. Halsaa, S. Roseneil and S. Sümer (eds) *Remaking Citizenship in Multicultural Europe: Women's Movements, Gender and Diversity*, Basingstoke: Palgrave Macmillan, pp 1–20.

Rubery, J. and Rafferty, A. (2014) 'Gender, recession and austerity in the UK', in M. Karamessini and J. Rubery (eds) *Women and Austerity*, London: Routledge, pp 123–43.

Sainsbury, D. (1996) *Gender, Equality and Welfare States*, Cambridge: Cambridge University Press.

Sainsbury, R. (2010) '21st century welfare—getting closer to radical benefit reform?', *Public Policy Research*, 17(2): 102–207.

Sainsbury, R. (2014) 'Talking Universal Credit: in conversation with Lord Freud, Minister for Welfare Reform', *Journal of Poverty and Social Justice*, 22(1): 37–44.

Saldaña, J. (2003) *Longitudinal Qualitative Research: Analyzing Change through Time*, Oxford: AltaMira Press.

Sevenhuijsen, S. (2000) 'Caring in the third way: the relation between obligation, responsibility and care in Third Way discourse', *Critical Social Policy*, 20(1): 5–37.

Skevik, A. (2005) 'Women's citizenship in the time of activation: the case of lone mothers in "needs-based" welfare states', *Social Politics*, 12(1): 42–66.

Smith, F., Barker, J., Wainwright, E., Marandet, E. and Buckingham, S. (2008) 'A new deal for single parents? Training single parents for work in West London', *Area*, 40(2): 237–44.

Smith, N. (2003) 'Cross-sectional profiling and longitudinal analysis: research notes on analysis in the longitudinal qualitative study, "Negotiating Transitions to Citizenship"', *International Journal of Social Research Methodology*, 6(3): 273–7.

SSAC (Social Security Advisory Committee) (2017) *In-work Progression and Universal Credit: A Study by the Social Security Advisory Committee. Occasional Paper No 19*, London: SSAC.

SSAC (2019) *The Effectiveness of the Claimant Commitment in Universal Credit: A Study by the Social Security Advisory Committee. Occasional Paper No 21*, London: SSAC.

Standing, G. (2011) 'Behavioural conditionality: why the nudges must be stopped – an opinion piece', *Journal of Poverty and Social Justice*, 19(1): 27–38.

Sung, S. and Bennett, F. (2007) 'Dealing with money in low-moderate income couples: insights from individual interviews', in K. Clarke, T. Maltby and P. Kennett (eds) *Social Policy Review 19: Analysis and Debate in Social Policy*, Bristol: Policy Press, pp 151–73.

Taylor-Gooby, P. (2012) 'Root and branch restructuring to achieve major cuts: the social policy programme of the 2010 UK Coalition government', *Social Policy and Administration*, 46(1): 61–82.

Thomas, A. and Griffiths, R. (2006) *Work Focused Interviews for Partners and Enhanced New Deal for Partners*, London: DWP.

Thomson, R. (2007) 'The qualitative longitudinal case history: practical, methodological and ethical reflections', *Social Policy and Society*, 6(4): 571–82.

Thompson, S. (2015) *The Low-pay, No-pay Cycle*, York: Joseph Rowntree Foundation.

Timmins, N. (2016) *Universal Credit: From Disaster to Recovery?* London: Institute for Government.

Toerien, M., Sainsbury, R., Drew, P. and Irvine, A. (2013) 'Putting personalisation into practice: work-focused interviews in Jobcentre Plus', *Journal of Social Policy*, 42(2): 309–27.

Tomlinson, J. (2006) 'Women's work-life balance trajectories in the UK: reformulating choice and constraint in transitions through part-time work across the life-course', *British Journal of Guidance and Counselling*, 34(3): 365–82.

Trickey, H. and Walker, R. (2001) 'Steps to compulsion within British labour market policies', in I. Lodemel and H. Trickey (eds) *'An Offer You Can't Refuse': Workfare in International Perspective*, Bristol: Policy Press, pp 181–213.

Tronto, J. (2001) 'Who cares? Public and private caring and the rethinking of citizenship', in N.J. Hirschmann and U. Liebert (eds) *Women and Welfare: Theory and Practice in the United States and Europe*, New Brunswick: Rutgers University Press, pp 65–83.

van den Berg, G.J. and Vikström, J. (2014) 'Monitoring job offer decisions, punishments, exit to work, and job quality', *The Scandinavian Journal of Economics*, 116(2): 284–334.

Veitch, J. and Bennett, F. (2010) *A Gender Perspective on 21st Century Welfare Reform*, Oxford: Oxfam Great Britain.

Vincent, C. (2017) '"The children have only got one education and you have to make sure it's a good one": parenting and parent–school relations in a neoliberal age', *Gender and Education*, 29(5): 541–57.

Walby, S. (1994) 'Is citizenship gendered?' *Sociology*, 28(2): 379–95.

Walker, C. (2018) 'Northern Powerhouse Livability Index', [online] Available from: www.yourhousinggroup.co.uk/media/1451/t-communications-public-relations-wpi-research-and-pr-artwork-final-artwork-northern-powerhouse-liveability-index-report.pdf [Accessed 22 August 2019].

Watts, B., Fitzpatrick, S., Bramley, G. and Watkins, D. (2014) *Welfare Sanctions and Conditionality in the UK*, York: Joseph Rowntree Foundation.

Webster, D. (2019) 'Briefing: benefit sanctions statistics. November 2019', *Child Poverty Action Group*, [online] Available from: https://cpag.org.uk/policy-and-campaigns/briefing/david-webster-university-glasgow-briefings-benefit-sanctions [Accessed 15 April 2020].

Whitworth, A. (2012) *Tailor Made? Single Parents' Experiences of Employment Support from Jobcentre Plus and the Work Programme*, London: Gingerbread.

Whitworth, A. and Griggs, J. (2013) 'Single parents and welfare-to-work conditionality: necessary, just, effective?', *Ethics and Social Welfare*, 7(2): 124–40.

Wickham, S., Bentley, L., Rose, T., Whitehead, M., Taylor-Robinson, D. and Barr, B. (2020) 'Effects on mental health of a UK welfare reform, Universal Credit: a longitudinal controlled study', *The Lancet Public Health*, 5(3), e157–e164. doi.org/10.1016/S2468-2667(20)30026-8

Williams, F. (2001) 'In and beyond New Labour: towards a new political ethics of care', *Critical Social Policy*, 21(4): 467–93.

Williams, F. (2004) *Rethinking Families*, London: Calouste Gulbenkain Foundation.

Williams, F. (2012) 'Care relations and public policy: social justice claims and social investment frames', *Families, Relationships and Societies*, 1(1): 103–19.

Wood, M. (2021) 'Childcare costs and Universal Credit: awareness, affordability and the challenge of an embedded system', *Journal of Poverty and Social Justice*, 29(2): 203–20.

Work and Pensions Committee (2012) *Universal Credit Implementation: Meeting the Needs of Vulnerable Claimants. Third Report of Session 2012–13*, London: House of Commons.

Work and Pensions Committee (2015) *Benefit Sanctions: Beyond the Oakley Review: Government Response to the Committee's Fifth Report of Session 2014–15. Third Special Report of Session 2015–16*, London: House of Commons.

Work and Pensions Committee (2016) *The Future of Jobcentre Plus: Second Report of Session 2016–17*, London: House of Commons.

Work and Pensions Committee (2017) *Universal Credit: The Six Week Wait. First Report of Session 2017–19*, London: House of Commons.

Work and Pensions Committee (2018a) *Benefit Sanctions: Nineteenth Report of Session 2017–19*, London: House of Commons.

Work and Pensions Committee (2018b) *Universal Credit: Childcare. Twenty-second Report of Session 2017–19*, London: House of Commons.

Work and Pensions Committee (2018c) *Universal Credit: Supporting Self-employment. Eleventh Report of Session 2017–19*, London: House of Commons.

Woudheysen, A. (2019) *Worse Off: The Impact of Universal Credit on Families in Tower Hamlets*, London: Child Poverty Action Group.

Wright, S. (2011) 'Relinquishing rights? The impact of activation on citizenship for single parents in the UK', in S. Betzelt and S. Bothfeld (eds) *Activation and Labour Market Reforms in Europe: Challenges to Social Citizenship*, Basingstoke: Palgrave Macmillan, pp 59–78.

Wright, S. (2012) 'Welfare-to-work, agency and personal responsibility', *Journal of Social Policy*, 41(2): 309–28.

Wright, S. and Dwyer, P. (2022) 'In-work Universal Credit: claimant experiences of conditionality mismatches and counterproductive benefit sanctions', *Journal of Social Policy*, 51(1): 20–38.

Wright, S. and Patrick, R. (2019) 'Welfare conditionality in lived experience: aggregating qualitative longitudinal research', *Social Policy and Society*, 18(4): 597–613.

Wright, S., Dwyer, P., Jones, K., McNeill, J., Scullion, L. and Stewart, A.B.R. (2018) Final Findings: Universal Credit, Welfare Conditionality, [online] Available from: www.welfareconditionality.ac.uk/wp-content/uploads/2018/05/40414-Universal-Credit-web.pdf [Accessed 30 October 2020].

Wright, S., Fletcher, D.R. and Stewart, A.B.R. (2020) 'Punitive benefit sanctions, welfare conditionality, and the social abuse of unemployed people in Britain: transforming claimants into offenders?' *Social Policy and Administration*, 54(2): 278–94.

York Human Rights (2018) York Human Rights Indicator Report: Human Rights: Reclaiming the Positive, York: Human Rights City, [online] Available from: www.yorkhumanrights.org/wp-content/uploads/2019/02/43502_Applied-Human-Rights-Booklet-LR3.pdf [Accessed 25 July 2019].

Young, I.M. (1995) 'Mothers, citizenship, and independence: a critique of pure family values', *Ethics*, 105(3): 535–56.

Yuval-Davis, N. and Werbner, P. (2005) 'Introduction: women and the new discourse of citizenship', in N. Yuval-Davis and P. Werbner (eds) *Women, Citizenship and Difference*, New Delhi: Zubaan, pp 1–38.

Index

References to figures appear in *italic* type; those in **bold** type refer to tables. References to footnotes show both the page number and the note number (3n1).
UC stands for Universal Credit. Other abbreviations are from page vii.

D

R

S

T

U

Printed and bound by CPI Group (UK) Ltd, Croydon, CR0 4YY
15/09/2026
14962386-0001